Edward Arber, William Webbe

A Discourse of English Poetrie. 1586

Edited by Edward Arber

Edward Arber, William Webbe

A Discourse of English Poetrie. 1586
Edited by Edward Arber

ISBN/EAN: 9783337011017

Printed in Europe, USA, Canada, Australia, Japan

Cover: Foto ©Thomas Meinert / pixelio.de

More available books at **www.hansebooks.com**

English Reprints.

WILLIAM WEBBE, Graduate.

A Discourse of English Poetrie.

1586.

CAREFULLY EDITED BY

EDWARD ARBER,

Associate, King's College, London, F.R.G.S., &c.

LONDON:
5 QUEEN SQUARE, BLOOMSBURY, W.

t. Stat. Hall.]   1 December, 1870.   [*All Rights reserved.*

CONTENTS.

NOTES of William **Webbe**,	3
CONTEMPORARY ENGLISH AUTHORS referred to,	5
INTRODUCTION,	7
BIBLIOGRAPHY,	10

A DISCOURSE OF ENGLISH POETRIE, — 11

1. The Epistle to Edward Sulyard, Esquire, . . 13
2. A Preface to the noble Poets of England, . . 17
3.   A DISCOURSE OF ENGLISH POETRIE, . 21
   - (a) What Poetry is? 21
   - (b) The beginning of Poetry, and of what estimation it hath always been, ... 21
   - (c) The use of Poetry, and wherein it rightly consisted, ... 25
   - (d) The Author's judgment of English Poets, . 30
   - (e) 𝔗𝔥𝔢 𝔐𝔞𝔱𝔱𝔢𝔯 𝔬𝔣 𝔈𝔫𝔤𝔩𝔦𝔰𝔥 𝔓𝔬𝔢𝔱𝔯𝔦𝔢, . . 38-56
     Ex. Comparison of Thomas Phaer's translation of the *Æneid* with the original text of Virgil.
   - (f) 𝔗𝔥𝔢 𝔐𝔞𝔫𝔫𝔢𝔯 𝔬𝔯 𝔉𝔬𝔯𝔪 𝔬𝔣 𝔈𝔫𝔤𝔩𝔦𝔰𝔥 𝔓𝔬𝔢𝔱𝔯𝔦𝔢, . 56-84
     - A. RHYMED VERSE.
       There be three special notes necessary to be observed in the framing of our accustomed English Rhyme:—
       - (1) *The metre or verse must be proportionate* . 57
         Ex. Criticism of the different sorts of Verse in Spencer's *Shepherds Calender*.
       - (2) *The natural Accent of the words must not be wrested* 62
       - (3) *The Rhyme or like ending of verses* . 63
     - B. The Reformed kind of ENGLISH VERSE [*i.e.*, in CLASSICAL FEET], . . . 67-84
       Ex. The Author's translation of the first two *Eglogues* of Virgil into English Hexameters, 73-79
       Ex. His translation of Hobbinoll's Song in the *Shepherds Calender* into English Sapphics, 81-84
   - (g) The Canons or general Cautions of Poetry, prescribed by Horace: collected by George Fabricius [*b.* 23 April 1516 at Chemnitz,—*d.* 13 July 1571] 85-95
4. EPILOGUE, ... 96

Notes
of
WILLIAM WEBBE.

* *Probable or approximate dates.*

Very little is known of the Author of this work. The suggestion that he was the William Webbe, M.A., one of the joint Authors of a topographical book *The Vale Royal*, 1648, fol., is quite anachronistic.

Messrs. Cooper, in *Athenæ Cantabrigiensis*, **ii. 12.** *Ed.* 1861, state that our Author "was a **graduate** of this University, but we have no **means of** determining his college. **One** of this name, who was of St. John's College, was B.A. 1572-3 [the **same** year as Spenser], **as was** another who was of Catharine Hall in **1581-2**. His place of residence is unknown, although it may perhaps **be inferred** that it was in or near the county of Suffolk. We have **no information as to** his position in life, or the time or place of his death. **He was** evidently a man of superior intellect and no mean attainments." [Our Author apparently witnessed *Tancred and Gismund* in 1568, **and** being evidently acquainted with Gabriel Harvey and Spenser (who left Cambridge in 1578), must be the earlier graduate of the above two Webbes.]

1568. *Tancred and Gismund*, written **by five members of** the Inner Temple, the first letters of whose names are attached to the several acts, viz., Rod. Staff; Hen. No[well?]; **G. A**ll; Ch. Hat[ton?]; and R. W[ilmot]: is 'curiously **acted in** view of her Maiesty, by whom it was then princely accepted.'

Webbe appears to have been present at the representation : see **1591**. Mr. J. P. Collier in his edition of 'Dodsley's *Old Plays*,' i. 153, prints from a MS. what is apparently **a** portion of this Tragedy as it was then acted, written in alternate rhymes. He also states in his *Hist. of Dram. Poet.* that it 'is the earliest English play extant, the plot of which **is known to be** derived from an Italian novel." *iii.* 13. *Ed.* **1831**.

***1572-3.** Our Author takes his B.A. at Cambridge.

1582. Nov. **28.** Gabriel Poyntz presented Robert Wilmott, **clerk to the** Rectory of North Okendon, Essex : 18 miles from **London**. *Newcourt Repertorium*, ii. 447. *Ed.* 1710.

Flemyngs is a large manor house in Essex in the **parish** of Runwell, in the hundred of Chelmsford ; from which town it is ten miles distant, and about twenty-nine miles from London. 'This house commands extensive views of some parts of the county and of Kent, including more than thirty parish churches.'

Edward Sulyard succeeded, on the death of his father Eustace in 1546, to Flemyngs and other possessions. He had two sons, Edward and Thomas, **and a** daughter named Elizabeth. He was knighted on 23 July 1603 at Whitehall by James I, before his coronation : and died in June 1610. Of his two sons, Edward died without issue; Thomas, *b.* **1573**, was knighted, and *d.* March 1634; leaving a son Edward, who *d.* **7** Nov. **1692** without issue, ' the last of **the** house and family.' See *W. Berry, County Gen. Essex*, 64. T. Wright, *Hist. of Essex*, i. 142, 143. *Ed.* 1831. J. P[hilipot] *Knts. Batch. made by James I.* 1660.

***1583** or **4.** Webbe appears to have been at this time private tutor to Mr. Sulyard's two sons, for he presented his MS. translation (now lost) of the *Georgics* to Mr. Sulyard : see *pp.* 55 and 16.

1585. Dec. 2. The Dean and Chapter of St. Paul's appoint Robert Wilmott, M.A., to the Vicarage of Horndon on the Hill, twenty-four miles from London, and a few miles from Flemyngs, where his friend Webbe was a private tutor. *Newcourt, idem.* ii. 343.

1586. Of '**the** pregnant ympes of right excellent hope,' Thomas Sulyard was about thirteen years old, and his brother Edward was older than him.

W. Webbe writes the present **work in** the summer evenings.

SEPT. 4. It is thus registered for **publication.**
  "Robt. Walley
  John Charlewood, **Rd. of them, for printinge A** Discourse of englishe poetrye . . . . . . vj^d."
  J. P. Collier, Extr. of Stat. **Co.'s Regrs. ii., 215. Ed** 1849.

1587. FEB. 5. Margaret, the mother of Mr. **Sulyard died. She is** buried at Runwell.

1588. Warton quotes "a small black-lettered tract **entitled** *The Touch-stone of Wittes,* chiefly compiled, with **some** slender additions, from William Webbe's *Discourse of English Poetrie,* written by Edward Hake, and printed **at London by** Edmund Bollifant." *p.* 804. *Ed.* 1870.

Our Author—his pupils growing to manhood—then appears to have **gone,** possibly also in the **same** capacity of private tutor into the family of **Henry** Grey, Esquire [created Baron Grey of Groby, 21 July 1603; *d.* 1614] at Pirgo, in the parish **of** Havering atte Bower, Essex: fifteen miles from London. Dugdale states that the first husband of one of the daughters of this Henry Grey, Esquire, was a *William Sulyard,* Esquire. *Baron. i.* 722. *Ed.* 1675. From this old Palace of the Queens of England Webbe wrote the following letter to Wilmott, which is **reprinted** in the revised edition of *Tancred and Gismund* published in 1592: **of** which there **are** copies in the Bodleian, and at Bridgewater House, and **an** imperfect **one** in the British Museum (C. 34, e. 44).

1591. AUG. 8. *To his frend R. W.* **Master** *R.* **VV. looke not now** for the tearmes of an intreator, **I** wil beg no longer, and **for** your promises, I wil refuse **them as** bad paiment: neither can I be satisfied with any thing, **but** a peremptorie performance of an old intention of yours, the publishing I meane of those wast **papers** (as it pleaseth you to cal them, but as **I** esteem them, **a** most exquisite inuention**)** of *Gismunds* Tragedie. Thinke **not to** shift me off with longer delayes, nor alledge more ex**cuses to** get further respite, least I arrest you with my *Actum est,* **and** commence such a Sute of vnkindenesse against you, **as** when the case shall be scand before the Iudges of courtesie, **the court** will crie out of your immoderat modestie. And thus much **I** tel you before, you shal not be able to wage against **me in the** charges growing **vpon** this action, especially, if the **worshipful** company of the **Inner** temple gentlemen patronize **my cause, as** vndoubtedly **they** wil, yea, and rather plead **partially for** me then let my cause miscary, because them**selues are** parties. The tragedie **was** by them most pithely **framed,** and **no** lesse curiously **acted in** view **of** her Maiesty, **by whom** it was then as princely accepted, as of the whole **honorable** audience notably applauded: yea, and of al men **generally** desired, **as a** work, **either in** statelines of shew, **depth of** conceit, **or** true ornaments **of** poeticall arte, inferior **to none of the** best in that kinde : **no,** were the Roman *Seneca* **the censurer.** The braue youths that then (to their high praises) so feelingly performed the same in action, did shortly after lay vp the booke vnregarded, or perhaps let it run abroade (as many parentes doe their children once past dandling) not respecting so much what hard fortune might befall it being out of their fingers, as how their heroical wits might againe be quickly conceiued with new inuentions of like worthines, wherof they haue been euer since wonderfull fertill. But this orphan of theirs (for he wandreth as it were fatherlesse,) hath notwithstanding, by the rare and bewtiful perfections appearing in him, hetherto neuer wanted great fauourers, and louing preseruers. Among whom I cannot sufficiently commend your more then charitable zeale, and scholerly compassion towards him, that haue not only rescued and defended him from the deuouring iawes of obliuion, but vouchsafed also to apparrel him in a new sute at your own charges, wherein he may again more boldly come abroad, and by your permission returne to his olde parents, clothed perhaps not in richer or more costly furniture than it went from them, but in handsomnes and fashion more answerable to these times, wherein fashions are so often altered. Let one word suffice for your encouragement herein: namely, your commendable pains in disrobing him of his antike curiositie, and adorning him with the approoued guise of our stateliest Englishe termes (not diminishing, but augmenting his artificiall colours of absolute poesie, deriued from his first parents) cannot but bee grateful to most mens appetites, who vpon our experience we know highly to esteem such lofty measures of sententiously composed Tragedies.

How much you shal make me, and the rest of your priuate frends beholding vnto you, I list not to discourse: and therefore grounding vpon these alledged reasons, that the suppressing of this Tragedie, so worthy for ye presse, were no other thing then wilfully to defraud your selfe of an vniuersall thank, your frends of their expectations, and sweete G. of a famous eternitie. I will cease to doubt of any other pretence to cloake your bashfulnesse, hoping to read it in print (which lately lay neglected amongst your papers) at our next appointed meeting.

I bid you heartely farewell. From Pyrgo in Essex, August the eight, 1591. *Tuus fide et facultate.* GUIL. WEBBE.

It may also be noted that Wilmott dedicated this revised tragedy to two Essex ladies: one of whom was Lady Anne Grey, the daughter of Lord Windsor, and the wife of the above-mentioned Henry Grey, Esquire of Pirgo.

That the above R. Wilmott, Clergyman, is the same as the Reviser of the play appears from the following passage in his Preface.

"Hereupon I have indured some conflicts between reason and judgement, whether it were convenient for the commonwealth, and the *indecorum* of my calling (as some think it) that the memory of *Tancred's* Tragedy should be again by my means revised, which the oftner I read over, and the more I considered thereon, the sooner I was won to consent thereunto: calling to mind that neither the thrice reverend and learned father, M. Beza, was ashamed in his younger years to send abroad, in his own name, his Tragedy of *Abraham*, nor that rare Scot (the scholar of our age) *Buchanan*, his most pathetical *Ieptha*." 'Dodsley's Old Plays,' ii. 165. Ed. by J. P. Collier, 1825.

If the identity may be considered as established, Wilmott the Poet lived on till 1619: when he was succeeded on his death by W. Jackson, in the Rectory of North Okendon. *Newcourt, idem.* ii. 447.

No later information concerning W. Webbe than the above letter, has yet been recovered.

CONTEMPORARY ENGLISH AUTHORS
REFERRED TO IN THE FOLLOWING *Difcourfe.*

G. B.	? *The Shippe of Safeguarde,* 1569 . .	35
F. C.	?	35
T. CHURCHYARD.	*Church*yard's '*Chippes*,' 1575; *Church*yard's '*Chance*,' 1580; *Churchyard*'s '*Charge*,' 1580	33
M. D.	[? Mafter Dyer, *i.e.*, Sir Edward Dyer] . .	33
? DARRELL	?	35

R. EDWARDES. *Par. of Dainty Devises*, 1576; *Comedies*	33
Sir T. ELYOT. *The Governor*, 1538	42, 43
G. GASCOIGNE. *Posies*, 1572; *The Steele Glas*, &c., 1576	33
B. GOOGE. *Eglogs, Epytaphes, and Sonettes*, 1563; translation of *Palingenius*	34
Sir J. GRANGE. *The Golden* **Aphroditis**, **1577**	35
G. HARVEY.	35
HEIWOOD [either JOHN HEYWOOD or JASPER HEYWOOD]	33
W. HUNNIS. *Paradise of Dainty* **Devises**, **1576, 1578**	33
? HYLL ?	33
E. K. [*i.e.* EDWARD KIRKE]	33, 53
F. K. [? Fr. Kindlemarsh] *Par. of Dainty* **Devises**, **1576, 1578**	35
J. LYLY. *Euphues*, 1579-80; *Plays*	46
A. MUNDAY. *The Mirrour of Mutabilitie*, **1579**; *The Paine of Pleasure*, 1580	35
T. NORTON. **Joint Author of** *Ferrex* and *Porrex*, 1561	33
C. OCKLANDE. *Anglorum Prælia*, 1580, 1582	30
[? DR. E.] SAND[YS]. **Par. of Dainty** *Devises*, **1576**, &c.	33
E. SPENSER. *Shepheards* **Calender**, **1579**, 1581, 1586	35, 52, 81
HENRY, Earl of SURREY. *Sonnets, &c.*, in *Tottel's Misc.* 1557	33
T. TUSSER. *Five* **hundred points of Good** *Husbandrie*, **1557-80**	33
THOMAS, Lord VAUX. *Sonnetes, &c.*, in *Tottel's Misc.* **1557**; and *Par. of Dainty Devises*, 1576	33
E. VERE, Earl of OXFORD. Unpublished *Sonnets*	33
G. WHETSTONE. *The Rocke of Regard*, 1576	35
R. WILMOTT. *Tancred and Gismund*, 1568	35
S. Y. [? M. YLOOP, *i.e.* M. POOLY in *Par. of Dainty Devises*]	33

THE TRANSLATORS.

SENECA.

J. HEYWOOD. *Troas*, 1559; *Thyestes*, 1560; *Hercules Furens*, 1561	34
A. NEVILL. *Œdipus*, 1563	34
J. STUDLEY. *Medea*, 1566; *Agamemnon*, 1566	34

OVID.

G. TURBERVILLE. *Heroical Epistles*, **1567**	34
A. GOLDING. *Metamorphoses*, 1565	34, 51
T. CHURCHYARD. *Tristia*, 1578	**34**
T. DRANT. *Satires*, **1566**; *Art of Poetrie*, 1567	**34**

VIRGIL.

HENRY, **Earl** of **SURREY**. *Two Books of the 'Æneid,'* 1557	33
T. PHAER, M.D. 9½*rd Books of the 'Æneid,'* 1558-**1562**	33, 46-51
T. TWYNE. *The remaining* 2⅔*rd Books*, 1573	34
A. FLEMING. *Bucolicks*, 1575, in rhyme. His *Georgics* referred to **at** *p.* 55 appeared in 1589	34, 55

A Discourse of English Poetrie

INTRODUCTION.

Apart from the excessive rarity of this work, two copies of it only being known; it deserves permanent republication as a good example of the best form of Essay Writing of its time; and as one of the series of Poetical Criticisms before the advent of Shakespeare as a writer, the study of which is so essential to a right understanding of our best Verse.

Although Poetry is the most ethereal part of Thought and Expression; though Poets must be born and cannot be made: yet is there an art of Poesy; set forth long ago by Horace but varying with differing languages and countries, and even with different ages in the life of the same country. In our tongue—Milton only excepted—there is nothing approaching, either in the average merit of the Journeymen or the superlative excellence of the few Master-Craftsmen, the Poesy of the Elizabethan age. Hence the value of these early Poetical Criticisms. Their discussion of principles is most helpful to all readers in the discernment of the subtle beauties of the numberless poems of that era: while for those who can, and who will; they will be found singularly suggestive in the training of their own Power of Song, for the instruction and delight of this and future generations.

A Cambridge graduate; the private tutor, for some two or three years past, to Edward and Thomas Sulyard, the sons of Edward Sulyard Esquire, of Flemyngs, situated in Essex, some thirty miles distant from London: our Author gave his leisure hours to the study of Latin and English poetry.

He had acquainted himself with our older Poets, and with the contemporary verse: and, thinking for himself, he endeavoured to see exactly what English poetry actually was, and what it might and should become. Doubtless in his walks in the large park surrounding the Old Manor House this subject often occupied his thoughts, and he sat down to commit his opinions to the press, in the presence and quietude of a large and fair landscape stretching far away southward beyond the Thames into Kent, diversified with the spires of many churches and the masts of many passing ships: and all illuminated with the glow and glory of the summer evenings of 1586.

Webbe was as much affected with the 'immoderate modesty' with which, five years later, he charged Wilmot, as any of the writers of that age. He dreads, at *p.* 55, the unauthorized publication of his version of the *Georgics,* and he must have been moved deeply by 'the rude multitude of rusticall Rymers, who will be called Poets' before he ventured to advocate in print 'the reformation of our English Verse,' *i.e.,* the abandonment of Rhyme for Metre.

He calls his work 'a sleight somewhat compiled for recreation in the intermyssions of my daylie businesse,' yet it is the most extensive piece of Poetical Criticism that had hitherto appeared. He had read, for he quotes at *p.* 64, G. Gascoigne's *Certayne Notes, &c.,* 1575: also *Three proper and wittie, familiar Letters,* by Immerito [Edmund Spenser] and G[abriel] H[arvey] 1580, to which he alludes at *p.* 36. He may have heard of Sir P. Sidney's *Apologie for Poetrie* [1582], then circulating in manuscript, or of the young Scotch King's *Reulis and Cautelis of Scottish Poesie,* then being

publifhed at Edinburgh. Yet none of thefe is fo
lengthy, nor deals with the fame extent of fubject,
nor is illuftrated by original examples, as is this
Difcourfe.

Though the book is an honeft one, faithfully repre-
fenting the author's robuft mind; it was written under
the ftrong influence of three works: Afcham's *Schole-
mafter*, 1570; Edwardes' *Paradife of Dainty Devices*,
1576; and Spenfer's *Shepherdes Calender*, anonymoufly
publifhed, without the author's confent, by E. K. [*i.e.*,
Edward Kirke, as is generally believed] in 1579. He
follows Afcham as to the origin of Rhyme; and alfo in
his error as to Simmias Rhodias at *p.* 57, &c. He quotes
W. Hunnis' poem at *p.* 66, from the collection of
Edwardes. It is alfo Webbe's great merit as a lover
and judge of poetry, that he inftinctively fixes upon
the *Shepherdes Calender* (never openly acknowledged
by Spenfer in his lifetime) as the revelation of a great
poet, as great an Englifh Poet indeed, as had yet appeared. That Paftoral Poem gave Webbe a higher
reverence for Spenfer than his great Allegory breeds
refpect for him in many, now-a-days.

The facility of Rhyme, at a time when there were many
wonderfully facile Rhymers, induced Afcham, Webbe,
and many others to feek after a more difficult form of
Englifh verfe. Claffical feet Webbe himfelf experienced to be a 'troublefome and unpleafant peece of
labour,' fo he fought after fomething more adapted to
the nature of the language, 'fome perfect platforme or
Profodia of verfifying.' Blank verfe would have fatif-
fied him, but he did not recognife its merits in Surrey's
tranflation of the *Æneid*. He is, however, warm in
his praife of Phaer's verfion of that work in hexameters: and gives us three pieces of reformed verfe of
his own coinage; two in hexameters, and one in
fapphics.

Finally, Webbe wrote 'thefe fewe leaues' 'to ftirre

vppe fome other of meete abilitie, to beftowe trauell in this matter.' His wifh had been anticipated. Already a Mafter Critic was at work—we know not for certainty whether it was George Puttenham, or who elfe—who, beginning to write in 1585, publifhed in 1589 *The Arte of Englifh Poefie*: which is the largeft and ableft criticifm of Englifh Poefy that appeared in print, during the reign of Elizabeth.

BIBLIOGRAPHY.

Issues in the Author's lifetime.

I.—*As a feparate publication.*

1. 1586. London. 1 vol. 4to. See title on oppofite page.

    Of the two copies known, the one here reprinted is among the Malone books in the Bodleian. The other paffed from hand to hand at the following fales: always increafing in price.
    1773. APR. 8. Mr. West's sale, No. 1856, 10s. 6d., to Mr. Pearson.
    1778. APR. 22. Mr. Pearson's sale, No. 1888, £3, 5s., to Mr. Stevens.
    1800. MAY 19. Mr Stevens' sale, No. 1128, £8, 8s., to the Duke of Roxburghe.
    1812. JUNE 2. The Roxburghe sale, No. 3168, £64, to the Marquis of Blandford.

Issues since the Author's death.

I.—*As a feparate publication.*

3. 1870. DEC. 1. London. *Englifh Reprints*: fee title at 1 vol. 8vo. *p.* 1.

    II.—*With other works.*

2. 1815. London. *Ancient Critical Effays.* Ed. by J. Haflewood. *A Difcourfe of Englifh Poetrie* occupies Vol. ii., *pp.* 13-95.

A Discourse of English Poetrie.

Together, with the Authors iudgment, touching the reformation of our English Verse.

By VVilliam VVebbe Graduate.

Imprinted at London, by Iohn Charlewood for Robert VValley
1 5 8 6.

To the right vvorſhip=
full, learned, and moſt gentle Gentle-
man, *my verie good* Master, Ma.
Edward Suliard, Eſquire. VV. VV.
wyſheth his harts deſire.

(∴)

Ay it pleaſe you Syr, *thys once more to beare with* my rudenes, *in preſenting* vnto *your viewe,* an other *ſlender conceite, of my ſimple capa̅ city: wherin although* I *am not able to bring* you *anie thing, which is meete to detaine* you *from your more ſerious matters: yet vppon* my *knowledge of your former courteſy and your fauourable countenaunce towardes all enterpriſes of Learning,* I *dare make bold to craue your accuſtomed patience, in turning* ouer *ſome of theſe fewe leaues, which* I *ſhall account* a greater *recompence, then the wryting thereof may deſerue.*

The Epistle.

The firme hope of your wonted gentlenes, not any good *lyking of myne owne labour, made me thus presumptuously to craue your worships patronage for my poore booke. A pretty aunswere is* **reported by** *some* **to** *be made by* Appelles **to** *King* Alexander, **who** *(in* **disport***) taking vp* **one** *of his pensilles to drawe a line, and asking the Paynters iudgment of his draught,* It is doone *(quoth* Apelles*)* like a King*: meaning indeede it was drawen* **as** *he pleased, but was nothing lesse then good workmanshippe. My selfe in like sort, taking vppon me, to make a draught of* English *Poetry, and requesting your worshyps censure* **of the** *same, you wyll perhaps gyue me thys* **verdict***,* It **was** doone like a Scholler, *meaning,* **as I** *could,* **but** *indeede more like to* **a** *learner, then one through* **grounded** *in Poeticall workmanship.*

Alexander *in drawing his lyne, leaned sometime too hard, otherwhyle too soft, as neuer hauing beene apprentice to the Arte: I in drawing this Poeticall discourse, make it some where to straight (leauing out the cheefe colloures and ornaments of Poetry) in an other place to wyde (stuffing in peeces little pertinent* **to true** *Poetry) as one neuer acquainted wyth the learned Muses.* What then? *as he being a king, myght meddle in what Scyence him listed, though therein hee had no skyll: so I beeing a learner, wyll trye my cunning in some parts of Learning, though neuer so simple.*

Nowe, as **for** *my saucie pressing vppon your expected* **fauor in crauing your** *iudgment, I beseech you let me* make thys excuse: that whereas true Gentilitie did neuer withdrawe her louing affection from Lady Learning, so I am perswaded, that your worshyppe cannot chuse, but continue your wonted fauourable benignitie towardes all the indeuourers to learning, of **which** corporation **I doo** indeede professe my selfe one sillie member.

For sith the wryters of all ages, haue sought as an vndoubted Bulwarke and stedfast sauegarde the patronage of Nobilitye, (a shielde as sure as can be to learning) wherin to shrowde and safelye place their seuerall inuentions: why should not I seeke some harbour for my poore trauell **to reste and staye** vppon, beeing of it selfe vnable to shyft the carping cauilles and byting scornes of lewde controllers?

And in trueth, where myght I rather choose a **sure** defence and readye refuge for the same, then where I see perfecte Gentilitye, and noblenesse of minde, **to** be faste lyncked with excellencie of learning and affable courtesye? Moreouer, adde thys **to** the **ende** of myne excuse: that I sende it into your sight, not as anie wyttie peece of worke **that may** delight you: but being a sleight somewhat compyled **for** recreation, in the intermyssions of my daylie businesse, (euen thys Summer Eueninges) as a token **of** that earnest and vnquenchable desyre I haue to shewe my selfe duetifull and welwylling towardes you. VVherevnto I am continually enflamed more and more, when I consider eyther your fauourable freendshyppe vsed towardes

my selfe, or your gentle countenaunce shewed to my simple
trauelles. The one I haue tryed in that homely translation I presented vnto you: the other I finde true in your
curteous putting to my trust, and dooing me so great
honesty and credite, with the charge of these towarde
young Gentlemen your sonnes.

   To which pregnant ympes **of** right excellent hope, I
would *I* were able, or you myght haue occasion to make
triall of my louing minde: who shoulde well perceyue my
selfe to remayne vnto them a faythfull and trusty Achates,
euen so farre **as** my wealth **my** woe, my power or perrill,
my penne or witte, my health **or** lyfe may serue to serche
myne ability.

   Huge heapes of wordes I myght pyle together to trouble
you withall: **eyther of my selfe or of** my dooinges, (as
some doo) or **of your** worshyppes commendable vertues (as
the moste doo) But I purposely chuse rather to let passe
the spreading of that worthy fame which you haue **euer**
deserued, then to runne in suspicion of fawning flattery
which I euer abhorred.

   Therefore once againe crauing your gentle pardon,
and patience in your ouerlooking thys rude
Epistle: and wyshing more happinesse then
my penne can expresse to you and your
whole retinewe, I rest.

(∴)

Your worshippes faithfull
                Seruant. VV. VV.

A Preface to the noble *Poets of Englande*.

Mong the innumerable fortes of Eng-lyſhe Bookes, and infinite fardles of printed pamphlets, wherewith thys Countrey is peſtered, all ſhoppes ſtuffed, and euery ſtudy furniſhed: the greateſt part I thinke in any one kinde, are ſuch as are either meere Poeticall, or which tende in ſome reſpecte (as either in matter or forme) to Poetry. Of ſuch Bookes therfore, ſith I haue beene one, that haue had a deſire to reade not the feweſt, and becauſe it is an argument, which men of great learning haue no ley-ſure to handle, or at leaſt hauing to doo with more ſerious matters doo leaſt regarde: If I write ſomething, concerning what I thinke of our Engliſh Poets, or ad-uenture to fette downe my ſimple iudgement of Engliſh Poetrie, I truſt the learned Poets will giue me leaue, and vouchſafe my Booke paſſage, as beeing for the rudeneſſe thereof no preiudice to their noble ſtudies, but euen (as my intent is) an *inſtar cotis* to ſtirre vppe ſome other of meete abilitie, to beſtowe trauell in this matter: whereby I thinke wee may not onelie get the meanes which wee yet want, to diſcerne betweene good writers and badde, but perhappes alſo challenge from the rude multitude of ruſticall Rymers, who will be called Poets, the right practiſe and orderly courſe of true Poetry.

It is to be wondred at of all, and is lamented of

manie, that where as all kinde of good learning, haue afpyred to royall dignitie and ſtatelie grace in our Engliſh tongue, being not onelie founded, defended, maintained, and enlarged, but alſo purged from faultes, weeded of errours, and polliſhed from barbarouſnes, by men of great authoritie and iudgement: onelie Poetrie hath founde feweſt frends to amende it, thoſe that can, referuing theyr ſkyll to themſelues, thoſe that cannot, running headlong vppon it, thinking to garniſh it with their deuiſes, but more corrupting it with fantaſticall errours. VVhat ſhoulde be the cauſe, that our Engliſh ſpeeche in ſome of the wyſeſt mens iudgements, hath neuer attained to anie ſufficient ripenes, nay not ful auoided the reproch of barbarouſnes in Poetry? the rudenes of the Countrey, or baſeneſſe of wytts: or the courſe *Dialect* of the ſpeeche? experience vtterlie diſproueth it to be anie of theſe: what then? ſurelie the canckred enmitie of curious cuſtome: which as it neuer was great freend to any good learning, ſo in this hath it grounded in the moſt, ſuch a negligent perſwaſion of an impoſſibilitie in matching the beſt, that the fineſt witts and moſt diuine heades, haue contented themſelues with a baſe kinde of fingering: rather debaſing theyr faculties, in ſetting forth theyr ſkyll in the courſeſt manner, then for breaking cuſtome, they would labour to adorne their Countrey and aduaunce their ſtyle with the higheſt and moſt learnedſt toppe of true Poetry. The rudenes or vnaptneſſe of our Countrey to be either none or no hinderaunce, if reformation were made accordinglie, the exquiſite excellency in all kindes of good learning nowe flouriſhing among vs, inferiour to none other nation, may ſufficiently declare.

The Preface.

That there be as sharpe and quicke wittes in England as euer were among the peerelesse Grecians, or renowmed Romaines, it were a note of no witte at all in me to deny. And is our speeche so course, or our phrase so harshe, that Poetry cannot therein finde a vayne whereby it may appeare like it selfe? why should we think so basely of this? rather then of her sister, I meane Rhetoricall *Eloquution*, which as they were by byrth Twyns, by kinde the same, by originall of one descent: so no doubt, as Eloquence hath founde such fauoures, in the English tongue, as she frequenteth not any more gladly: so would Poetrye if there were the like welcome and entertainment gyuen her by our English Poets, without question aspyre to wonderfull perfection, and appeare farre more gorgeous and delectable among vs. Thus much I am bolde to say in behalfe of Poetrie, not that I meane to call in question the reuerend and learned workes of Poetrie, written in our tongue by men of rare iudgement, and most excellent Poets: but euen as it were by way of supplication to the famous and learned Lawreat Masters of Englande, that they would but consult one halfe howre with their heauenly Muse, what credite they might winne to theyr natiue speeche, what enormities they might wipe out of English Poetry, what a fitte vaine they might frequent, wherein to shewe forth their worthie faculties: if English Poetrie were truely reformed, and some perfect platforme or *Prosodia* of versifying were by them ratifyed and sette downe: eyther in immitation of Greekes and Latines, or where it would skant abyde the touch of theyr Rules, the like obseruations selected and established by the naturall affectation of the speeche. Thus much I say, not to perswade you that are the fauourers of Englishe Poetry but to mooue it to you: beeing not the firste that haue thought vpon this matter, but one that by confent of others, haue taken vppon me to lay it once again in your wayes, if perhaps you may ftumble vppon it, and chance to looke fo lowe from your diuine cogitations, when your Mufe mounteth to the ftarres, and ranfacketh the Spheres of heauen: whereby perhaps you may take compaffion of noble Poetry, pittifullie mangled and defaced, by rude fmatterers and barbarous immitatours of your worthy ftudies. If the motion bee worthy your regard it is enough to mooue it, if not, my wordes woulde fimply preuaile in perfwading you, and therefore I reft vppon thys onely requeft, that of your courtefies, you wyll graunt paffage, vnder your fauourable corrections, for this my fimple cenfure of Englifh Poetry, wherein if you pleafe to runne it ouer, you fhall knowe breefely myne opinion of the moft part of your accuftomed Poets and particularly, in his place, the lyttle fomewhat which I haue fifted out of my weake brayne concerning thys reformed verfifying.

VV: VV;

A Discourse of Eng= lishe Poetrie.

Ntending to write some discourse of Englifh Poetrie, I thinke it not amyſſe if I ſpeake ſomething generally of Poetrie, as, what it is, whence it had the beginning, and of what eſtimation it hath alwayes beene and ought to be among al ſorts of people. Poetrie called in Greeke ποετρια, beeing deriued from the Verbe ποίεω, which ſignifieth in Latine *facere*, in Engliſh, to make, may properly be defined, the arte of making: which word as it hath alwaies beene eſpecially vſed of the beſt of our Engliſh Poets, to expreſſe ye very faculty of ſpeaking or wryting Poetically, ſo doth it in deede containe moſt fitly the whole grace and property of the ſame, ye more fullye and effectually then any other Engliſh Verbe. That Poetry is an Arte, (or rather a more excellent thing then can be contayned wythin the compaſſe of Arte) though I neede not ſtande long to prooue, both the witnes of *Horace*, who wrote *de arte Poetica*, and of *Terence*, who calleth it *Artem Muſicam*, and the very naturall property thereof may ſufficiently declare: The beginning of it as appeareth by *Plato*, was of a vertuous and moſt deuout purpoſe,

who witnesseth, that by occasion of meeting of a great company of young men, to solemnize ye feasts which were called *Panegeryca*, and were wont to be celebrated euery fift yeere, there, they that were most pregnant in wytt, and indued with great gyfts of wysedome and knowledge in Musicke aboue the rest did vse commonly to make goodly verses, measured according to the sweetest notes of Musicke, containing the prayse of some noble vertue, or of immortalitie, or of some such thing of greatest estimation: which vnto them seemed, so heauenly and ioyous a thing, that, thinking such men to be inspyrde with some diuine instinct from heauen, they called them *Vates*. So when other among them of the finest wits and aptest capacities beganne in imitation of these to frame ditties of lighter matters, and tuning them to the stroake of some of the pleasantest kind of Musicke, then began there to grow a distinction and great diuersity betweene makers and makers. Whereby (I take it) beganne thys difference: that they which handled in the audience of the people, graue and necessary matters, were called wise men or eloquent men, which they meant by *Vates*: and the rest which sange of loue matters, or other lighter deuises alluring vnto pleasure and delight, were called *Poetæ* or makers. Thus it appeareth, both Eloquence and Poetrie to haue had their beginning and originall from these exercises, beeing framed in such sweete measure of sentences and pleasant harmonie called $P\iota\theta\mu os$, which is an apt composition of wordes or clauses, drawing as it were by force ye hearers eares euen whether soeuer it lysteth: that *Plato* affirmeth therein to be contained λοητεία an inchauntment, as it were to perswade them anie thing whether they would or no. And heerehence is sayde, that men were first withdrawne from a wylde and sauadge kinde of life, to ciuillity and gentlenes, and ye right knowledge of humanity by the force of this measurable or tunable speaking.

This opinion shall you finde confirmed throughout

the whole workes of *Plato* and *Ariſtotle*. And that ſuch was the eſtimation of this Poetry at thoſe times, that they ſuppoſed all wiſedome and knowledge to be included myſtically in that diuine inſtinction, wherewith they thought their *Vates* to bee inſpyred. Wherevpon, throughout the noble workes of thoſe moſt excellent Philoſophers before named, are the authorities of Poets very often alledged. And *Cicero* in his *Tuſculane* queſtions is of that minde, that a Poet cannot expreſſe verſes aboundantly, ſufficiently, and fully, neither his eloquence can flowe pleaſauntly, or his wordes founde well and plenteouſly, without celeſtiall inſtinction: which Poets themſelues doo very often and gladlie witnes of themſelues, as namely *Ouid* in. 6. *Faſto*: *Est deus in nobis Agitante calleſcimus illo. etc.* Wherevnto I doubt not equally to adioyne the authoritye of our late famous Engliſh Poet, who wrote the *Sheepheards Calender*, where lamenting the decay of Poetry, at theſe dayes, ſaith moſt ſweetely to the ſame.

Then make thee winges of thine aſpyring wytt,

And whence thou cameſt flye back to heauen apace. etc.

Whoſe fine poeticall witt, and moſt exquiſite learning, as he ſhewed aboundantly in that peece of worke, in my iudgment inferiour to the workes neither of *Theocritus* in Greeke, nor *Virgill* in Latine, whom hee narrowly immitateth: ſo I nothing doubt, but if his other workes were common abroade, which are as I thinke in ye cloſe cuſtodie of certaine his freends, we ſhould haue of our owne Poets, whom wee might matche in all reſpects with the beſt. And among all other his workes whatſoeuer, I would wyſh to haue the ſight of hys *Engliſh Poet*, which his freend *E. K.* did once promiſe to publiſhe, which whether he performed or not, I knowe not, if he did, my happe hath not beene ſo good as yet to ſee it.

But to returne to the eſtimation of Poetry. Beſides ye great and profitable fruites contained in Poetry, for the inſtruction of manners and precepts of good life (for that was cheefly reſpected in the firſt age of Poetry) this is alſo added to the eternall commendations of that noble faculty: that Kinges and Princes, great and famous men, did euer encourage, mayntaine, and reward Poets in al ages: becauſe they were thought onely to haue the whole power in their handes, of making men either immortally famous for their valiaunt exploytes and vertuous exerciſes, or perpetually infamous for their vicious liues. Wherevppon it is ſaid of *Achilles*, that this onely vantage he had of *Hector*, that it was his fortune to be extolled and renowned by the heauenly verſe of *Homer*. And as *Tully* recordeth to be written of *Alexander*, that with natural teares he wept ouer *Achilles* Tombe, in ioy that he conceiued at the conſideration, howe it was his happe to be honoured wyth ſo diuine a worke, as *Homers* was. *Ariſtotle*, a moſt prudent and learned Philoſopher, beeing appointed Schoolemaſter to the young Prince *Alexander*, thought no worke ſo meete to be reade vnto a King, as the worke of *Homer*: wherein the young Prince being by him inſtructed throughly, found ſuch wonderfull delight in the ſame when hee came to maturity, that hee would not onely haue it with him in all his iourneyes, but in his bedde alſo vnder his pyllowe, to delight him and teache him both nights and dayes. The ſame is reported of noble *Scipio*, who finding the two Bookes of *Homer* in the ſpoyle of Kyng *Darius*, eſteemed them as wonderfull precious Iewelles, making one of them his companion for the night, the other for the day. And not onely was he thus affected to yat one peece or parte of Poetry, but ſo generally he loued the profeſſors thereof, that in his moſt ſerious affayres, and hotteſt warres againſt *Numantia* and *Carthage* he could no whitte be without that olde Poet *Ennius* in his company. But to ſpeake of all thoſe noble and wyſe Princes, who bare ſpeciall fauour and countenaunce to Poets, were tedious, and would require a rehearſall of all ſuch, in whoſe time there grewe any to credite and eſtimation in that faculty. Thus farre therefore may ſuffice for the eſtimation of Poets. **Nowe** I thinke moſt meete, to ſpeake ſomewhat, concerning what hath **beene** the vſe of Poetry, and wherin it rightly conſiſted, and whereof conſequently it obteyned **ſuch eſtimation.**

To begin therefore with the firſt that was **firſt worthe-lye memorable in** the excellent gyft of Poetrye, **the** beſt wryters **agree** that it was *Orpheus*, who by the ſweete gyft **of his heauenly** Poetry, withdrew men from raungyng **vncertainly, and wandring** brutiſhly about, and made **them gather together,** and keepe **company,** made houſes, **and** kept fellowſhippe together, **who** therefore is reported (as *Horace* ſayth) to aſſwage the fierceneſſe **of** Tygers, **and mooue** the harde Flynts. After him was *Amphion,* who **was the firſt that** cauſed **Citties to bee** builded, and men **therein to liue decently and** orderly according to lawe **and right.** Next, was *Tyrtæus*, who began to practiſe warlike **defences, to** keepe back enemies, and ſaue themſelues **from inuaſion** of foes. In thys place **I** thinke were **moſt conuenient** to rehearſe that auncient Poet *Pyndarus*: **but of the** certaine **time** wherein he flouriſhed, **I am not very** certaine: **but of the place** where he continued **moſte,** it ſhoulde ſeeme to **be the** Citty of *Thebes,* **by** *Plinie* who reporteth, that *Alexander* in ſacking **the ſame** Cittie, woulde not ſuffer **the** houſe wherein he dwelt **to** be ſpoyled as all the reſt were. **After theſe** was *Homer,* who as it were **in** one ſumme comprehended all know-**ledge,** wiſedome, learning, **and** pollicie, that was inci-dent to the capacity of man. **And who** ſo liſte to take viewe of hys two Bookes, one **of his** *Iliades*, the **other** his *Odiſsea,* ſhall throughly **perceiue** what the right vſe **of Poetry is: which** indeede **is to** mingle profite **with** pleaſure, **and ſo to** delight the Reader with **pleaſantnes** of hys Arte, as **in** ye meane time, his mind **may be well** inſtructed **with** knowledge and wiſedome. **For ſo** did that worthy Poet frame thoſe his two workes, that in reading the **firſt,** that is his *Iliads,* **by** declaring and ſetting forth **ſo** liuely **the Grecians** aſſembly againſt

Troy, together with their prowesse and fortitude againſt their foes, **a** Prince **ſhall** learne **not** onely courage, and valiantneſſe, but diſcretion alſo and pollicie to encounter with **his** enemies, yea a perfect forme **of wyſe** conſultations, with **his Captaines,** and exhortations **to** the people, with other **infinite** commodities.

Agayne, **in the other** part, wherein are deſcribed the manifold and daungerous aduentures of *Vliſſes*, **may a** man learne **many** noble vertues: and alſo **learne** to **eſcape** and **auoyde** the ſubtyll practiſes, and **perrilous entrappinges of** naughty perſons: and not onely **this, but in what ſort** alſo he may deale to knowe and per**ceiue the affections** of thoſe which **be neere** vnto him, **and moſt familiar with him,** the better to **put** them in **truſt** with **his matters of** waight and importaunce. Therefore **I** may boldly ſette downe thys to **be the trueſt, auncienteſt** and beſt kinde **of** Poetry, **to** direct **ones** endeuour **always** to that marke, that with delight **they may euermore adioyne** commoditie to theyr Readers: **which becauſe I** grounde vpon *Homer* the **Prince of all Poets, therefore haue I** alledged the order **of his worke, as an** authority ſufficiently proouing **this** aſſertion.

Nowe **what other Poets which followed him,** and **beene** of greateſt fame, haue doone for the moſte **parte in** their feuerall workes I wyll briefely, and **as my ſlender ability wyll** ſerue me declare. But by **my leaue, I muſt** content my ſelfe to ſpeake not **of** all, but of ſuch **as my** ſelfe haue ſeene, and beene beſt acquainted **withall, and** thoſe not **all** nor **the moſte** part of the **auncient** Grecians, of whom **I know not** how many there **were, but** theſe of the **Latiniſts,** which are of **greateſt fame and** moſt **obuious among vs.**

Thus much **I can** ſay, that *Ariſtotle* reporteth none **to haue greatly** flouriſhed **in Greece,** at leaſt wyſe **not left** behynd **them any** notable memoriall, **before** the **time** of *Homer.* **And** *Tully* ſayth as much, **that** there were none wrytt **woorth** the reading twyce in the Romaine tongue, before ye Poet *Ennius*. And ſurely as the very fumme or cheefeft effence of Poetry, dyd alwayes for the moft part confift in delighting the readers or hearers wyth pleafure, fo as the number of Poets increafed, they ftyll inclyned thys way rather then the other, fo that moft of them had fpeciall regarde, to the pleafantneffe of theyr fine conceytes, whereby they might drawe mens mindes into admiration of theyr inuentions, more then they had to the profitte or commoditye that the Readers fhoulde reape by their works. And thus as I fuppofe came it to paffe among them, that for the moft part of them, they would not write one worke contayning fome ferious matter: but for the fame they wold likewife powre foorth as much of fome wanton or laciuious inuention. Yet fome of the auncienteft fort of Grecians, as it feemeth were not fo much difpofed to vayne delectation: as *Ariftotle* fayth of *Empedocles*, that in hys iudgment he was onely a naturall Philofopher, no Poet at all, nor that he was like vnto *Homer* in any thing but hys meeter, or number of feete, that is, that hee wrote in verfe. After the time of *Homer*, there began the firfte Comedy wryters, who compyled theyr workes in a better ftile which continued not long, before it was expelled by penalty, for fcoffing too broade at mens manners, and the priuie reuengements which the Poets vfed againft their ill wyllers. Among thefe was *Eupolis*, *Cratinus*, and *Ariftophenes*, but afterward the order of thys wryting Comedies was reformed and made more plaufible: then wrytte *Plato*, *Comicus*, *Menander*, and I knowe not who more.

There be many moft profitable workes, of like antiquity, or rather before them, of the Tragedy writers: as of *Euripides*, and *Sophocles*, then was there *Phocitides* and *Theagines*, with many other: which Tragedies had their inuention by one *Thefpis*, and were pollifhed and amended by *Æfchilus*. The profitte or difcommoditie which aryfeth by the vfe of thefe Comedies and Tragedies, which is moft, hath beene long in controuerfie, and is fore vrged among vs at thefe dayes: what

I thinke of the same, perhaps I shall breefely declare anon.

Nowe concerning the Poets which wrote in homely manner, as they pretended, but indeede, with great pythe and learned iudgment, such as were the wryters of Sheepeheards talke and of husbandly precepts, who were among the Grecians that excelled, besides *Theocritus* and *Hesiodus* I know not, of whom the first, what profitable workes he left to posterity, besides hys *Idillia* or contentions of Goteheards, tending most to delight, and pretty inuentions, I can not tell. The other, no doubt for his Argument he tooke in hande, dealt very learnedly and profitably, that is, in precepts of Husbandry, but yet so as he myxed much wanton stuffe among the rest.

The first wryters of Poetry among the Latines, shoulde seeme to be those, which excelled in the framing of Commedies, and that they continued a long time without any notable memory of other Poets. Among whom, the cheefest that we may see or heare tell of, were these. *Ennius*, *Cæcilius*, *Næuius*, *Licinius*, *Attilius*, *Turpitius*, **Trabea**, *Luscius*, *Plautus*, and *Terens*. Of whom these two last named, haue beene euer since theyr time most famous, and to these dayes are esteemed, as greate helpes and furtheraunces to the obtayning of good Letters. But heere cannot I staye to speake of the most famous, renowned and excellent, that euer writte among the Latine Poets, *P. Virgill*, who performed the very same in that tongue, which *Homer* had doone in Greeke: or rather better if better might as *Sex. Propert.* in his *Elegies* gallantly recordeth in his praise, *Nescio quid magis nascitur Iliade*. Vnder the person of *Æneas* he expresseth the valoure of a worthy Captaine and valiaunt Gouernour, together with the perrilous aduentures of warre, and polliticke deuises at all assayes. And as he immitateth *Homer* in that worke, so dooth he likewyse followe the very steps of *Theocritus*, in his most pythy inuentions of his *Æglogues*: and likewyse *Hesiodus* in his *Georgicks* or bookes of

Englifh Poetrie.

Hufbandry, but yet more grauely, and in a more decent ftyle. But notwithftanding hys fage grauity and wonderfull wifedome, dyd he not altogether reftrayne his vayne, but that he would haue a caft at fome wanton and fkant comely an Argument, if indeede fuch trifles as be fathered vppon him were his owne. There followed after him, very many rare and excellent Poets, whereof the moft part writt light matters, as *Epigrammes* and *Elegies*, with much pleafant dalliance, among whom may be accounted *Propertius*, *Tibullus*, *Catullus*, with diuers whom *Ouid* fpeaketh of in diuers places of his workes. Then are there two Hyftoricall Poets, no leffe profitable then delightfome to bee read: *Silius* and *Lucanus*: the one declaring the valiant proweffe of two noble Captaines, one enemie to the other, that is, *Scipio* and *Haniball*: the other likewife, the fortitude of two expert warriours (yet more lamentably then the other becaufe thefe warres were ciuill) *Pompey* and *Cæfar*. The next in tyme (but as moft men doo account, and fo did he himfelfe) the fecond in dignity, we will ad ioyne *Ouid*, 'a moft learned, and exquifite Poet. The worke of greateft profitte which he wrote, was his Booke of *Metamorphofis*, which though it confifted of fayned Fables for the moft part, and poeticall inuentions, yet beeing moralized according to his meaning, and the trueth of euery tale beeing difcouered, it is a worke of exceeding wyfedome and founde iudgment. If one lyft in like manner, to haue knowledge and perfect intelligence of thofe rytes and ceremonies which were obferued after the Religion of the Heathen, no more profitable worke for that purpofe, then his bookes *De fastis*. The reft of his dooinges, though they tende to the vayne delights of loue and dalliaunce (except his *Tristibus* wherein he bewayleth hys exile) yet furely are mixed with much good counfayle and profitable leffons if they be wifely and narrowly read. After his time I know no worke of any great fame, till the time of *Horace*, a Poet not of the fmootheft ftyle, but in fharpneffe of wytt inferiour to none, and one to whom all the reſt both before his time and ſince, are very much beholding. About the ſame time *Iuuenall* and *Perſius*, then *Martial*, *Seneca* a moſt excellent wryter of Tragedies, *Boetius*, *Lucretius*, *Statius*, **Val**: **Flaccus**, **Ma***nilius*, *Auſonius*, *Claudian*, and many other, whoſe iuſt times and ſeuerall woorkes to ſpeake of in this place, were neither much needefull, nor altogeather tollerable, becauſe I purpoſed an other argument. Onely I will adde two of later times, yet not farre inferiour to the moſt of them aforeſayde, *Pallengenius*, and *Bap. Mantuanus*, and for a ſinguler gyft in a ſweete Heroicall verſe, match with them *Chr. Oclan.* the Authour of our *Anglorum Prælia*. But nowe leaſt I ſtray too farre from my purpoſe, I wyl come to our Engliſh Poets, to whom I would I were able to yeelde theyr deſerued commendations: and affoorde them that cenſure, which I know many woulde, which can better, if they were nowe to write in my ſteede.

I know no memorable worke written by any Poet in our Engliſh ſpeeche, vntill twenty yeeres paſt: where although Learning was not generally decayde at any time, eſpecially ſince the Conqueſt of King *William* Duke of *Normandy*, as it may appeare by many famous works and learned bookes (though not of this kinde) wrytten by Byſhoppes and others: yet ſurelye that Poetry was in ſmall price among them, it is very manifeſt, and no great maruayle, for euen that light of Greeke and Latine Poets which they had, they much contemned, as appeareth by theyr rude verſifying, which of long time was vſed (a barbarous vſe it was) wherin they conuerted the naturall property of the ſweete Latine verſe, to be a balde kinde of ryming, thinking nothing to be learnedly written in verſe, which fell not out in ryme, that is, in wordes whereof the middle worde of eche verſe ſhould ſound a like with the laſt, or of two verſes, the ende of both ſhould fall in the like letters as thus.

O male viuentes, verſus audite ſequentes.

English Poetrie.

And thus likewyfe.

> *Propter hæc et alia dogmata doctorum*
> *Reor effe melius et magis decorum:*
> *Quifque fuam habeat, et non proximorum.*

This brutifh **Poetrie**, though it had not the beginning in this Countrey, yet fo hath it beene affected heere, that the infection thereof would neuer (nor I thinke euer will) be rooted vppe againe: I meane this tynkerly verfe which we call ryme: Mafter *Afcham* fayth, that it firft began to be followed and maintained among the *Hunnes* and *Gothians*, and other barbarous Nations, who with the decay of all good learning, brought it into *Italy*: from thence it came into *Fraunce*, and fo to *Germany*, at laft conueyed into *England*, by men indeede of great wifedome and learning, but not confiderate nor circumfpect in that behalfe. But of this I muft intreate more heereafter.

Henry the firft King of that name in England, is wonderfully extolled, in all auncient Recordes of memory, for hys finguler good learning, in all kinde of noble ftudies, in fo much as he was named by his furname *Beaucleark*, as much to fay, as *Fayreclerke* (whereof perhappes came ye name of *Fayreclowe*) what knowledge hee attained in the fkyll of Poetry, I am not able to fay, I report his name for proofe, that learning in this Country was not little efteemed of at that rude time, and that like it is, among other ftudies, a King would not neglect the faculty of Poetry. The firft of our Englifh Poets that I haue heard of, was *Iohn Gower*, about the time of king *Rychard* the feconde, as it fhould feeme by certayne coniectures bothe a Knight, and queftionleffe a finguler well learned man: whofe workes I could wyfh they were all whole and perfect among vs, for no doubt they contained very much deepe knowledge and delight: which may be gathered by his freend *Chawcer*, who fpeaketh of him oftentimes, in diuer[s] places of hys workes. *Chawcer*, who for that excellent fame which hee **obtayned** in his Poetry, was alwayes accounted the **God of** Englifh Poets (fuch a tytle for honours fake hath beene giuen him) was next after, if not equall in time to *Gower*, and hath left many workes, both for delight and profitable **knowledge**, farre exceeding any other that as yet euer fince hys time directed theyr ftudies that way. Though the manner of hys ftile may feeme blunte and courfe to many fine Englifh eares at thefe dayes, yet in trueth, if it be equally pondered, and with good iudgment aduifed, **and confirmed** with the time wherein he wrote, a man **fhall perceiue thereby euen a true** picture or perfect fhape of a right Poet. He by his delightfome vayne, fo gulled the eares of men with his deuifes, **that**, although corruption bare fuch fway in moft matters, that learning and truth might fkant bee admitted to fhewe it felfe, yet without controllment, myght hee gyrde at the vices and abufes of all ftates, and gawle with very fharpe and eger inuentions, which he did fo learnedly and pleafantly, that none therefore would call **him** into queftion. For fuch was his bolde fpyrit, that what enormities he faw in any, he would not fpare to pay them home, eyther in playne words, **or els in fome** prety and pleafant couert, that the fimpleft might efpy him.

Neere in time vnto him was *Lydgate* a Poet, furely for good proportion of his **verfe**, and meetely currant **ftyle**, as the time affoorded comparable with *Chawcer*, yet more occupyed in fuperfticious and odde matters, then was requefite in fo good a wytte: which, though he handled them commendably, yet the matters themfelues beeing not fo commendable, hys eftimation hath beene the leffe. The next of our auncient Poets, that I can tell of, I fuppofe to be *Pierce Ploughman*, who in hys dooinges is fomewhat harfhe and obfcure, but indeede a very pithy wryter, and (to hys commendation I fpeake it) was the firft that I haue feene, that obferued ye quantity of our verfe without the curiofity of Ryme.

Since thefe **I** knowe none **other** tyll the time of

Skelton, who writ in the time of Kyng *Henry* the eyght, who as indeede he obtayned the Lawrell Garland, so may I wyth good ryght yeelde him the title of a Poet: hee was doubtles a pleasant conceyted fellowe, and of a very sharpe wytte, exceeding bolde, and would nyppe to the very quicke where he once sette holde. Next hym I thynke I may place master *George Gaskoyne*, as painefull a Souldier in the assayres of hys Prince and Country, as he was a wytty Poet in his wryting: whose commendations, becaufe I found in one of better iudgment then my selfe, I wyl sette downe hys wordes, and suppresse myne owne, of hym thus wryteth *E. K.* vppon the ninth *Æglogue* of the new Poet.

Master *George Gaskoyne* a wytty Gentleman and the very cheefe of our late rymers, who and if some partes of learning wanted not (albeit is well knowne he altogether wanted not learning) no doubt would haue attayned to the excellencye of those famous Poets. For gyfts of wytt, and naturall promptnes appeare in him aboundantly. I might next speake of the dyuers workes of the olde Earle of *Surrey*: of the L. *Vaus*, of *Norton*, of *Briftow*, **Edwardes**, *Tuffer*, *Churchyard*. **VVyl**: **Hunnis**: **Haiwood**: **Sand**: *Hyll*: *S. Y. M. D.* and many others, but to speake of their feuerall gyfts, and aboundant skyll shewed forth by them in many pretty and learned workes, would make my difcourfe much more tedious.

I may not omitte the deferued commendations of many honourable and noble **Lordes, and** Gentlemen, in her Maiesties Courte, which in the rare deuifes of Poetry, haue beene and yet are most excellent skylfull, among whom, the right honourable Earle of *Oxford* may challenge to him felfe the tytle of ye most excellent among the rest. I can no longer forget those learned Gentlemen which tooke such profitable paynes in translating the Latine Poets into our English tongue, whose defertes in that behalfe are more then I can vtter. Among thefe, I euer efteemed, and while I lyue, in my conceyt I shall account Master *D. Phaer*: without doubt the best: who as indeede hee had the best peece of **Poetry** whereon to sette a **most** gallant verse, so performed he it accordingly, **and in such sort,** as in my conscience I thinke would scarcely be doone againe, if it were to doo again. Notwithstanding, I speak it but as myne own fancy, **not preiudiciall to those that** list to thinke otherwyse. Hys worke whereof I speake, is the englishing of *Æneidos* of *Virgill*, so farre **soorth as it** pleased God **to** spare **him life,** which was **to the halfe** parte of the tenth Booke, the rest beeing since **wyth no lesse commendations** finished, **by** that worthy **scholler and famous Phisition** Master *Thomas Twyne.*

Equally with him may I well adioyne Master *Arthur Golding*, for hys labour in englishing *Ouids Metamorphosis*, for which Gentleman, **surely our** Country hath **for** many **respects** greatly **to gyue God thankes:** as for him which **hath** taken infinite **paynes without** ceasing, trauelleth as yet indefatigably, **and is addicted** without sociery, by **his** continuall laboure, **to profit** this **nation and** speeche **in all kind of** good **learning.** The next, very **well deserueth Master** *Barnabe Googe* to be **placed,** as a painefull **furtherer of** learning: hys **helpe to Poetry** besides hys **owne deuises, as** the translating of *Pallengenius. Lodiac.* **Abraham** *Flemming* as **in many prety Poesis of** hys **owne, so** in translating hath **doone to hys commendations.** To whom I would heere adioyne **one of hys name, whom** I know **to** haue excelled, **as well in all kinde of learning as in Poetry most especially, and would appeare so, if the dainty morselles,** and fine **poeticall inuentions of hys, were as common** abroade **as I knowe they be among** some of hys freendes. I wyl craue leaue of the laudable **Authors of** *Seneca* in English, **of the other** partes of *Ouid*, **of** *Horace*, of *Mantuan*, **and diuers other,** because **I would** hasten to ende thys rehearsall, perhappes offensyue **to** some, whom eyther by forgetfulnes, **or want of knowledge,** I must needes **ouer passe.**

And once againe, I am humbly to desire pardon of the learned company of Gentlemen Schollers, and

Englifh Poetrie.   35

ftudents of the Vniuerfities, and **Innes** of Courte, yf I omitte theyr feuerall commendations in this place, which I knowe a great number of them haue worthely deferued, in many rare **deuifes**, and finguler inuentions of Poetrie: for neither hath it beene my good happe, to haue feene all which I haue hearde of, neyther is my abyding in fuch place, where I can with facility get knowledge of their workes.

One Gentleman **notwithftanding** among them **may** I not ouerflyppe, fo farre reacheth his fame, and fo worthy is he, if hee haue not already, to weare the Lawrell wreathe, Mafter *George VVhetftone*, a man fingularly well fkyld in this faculty of Poetrie: To him I wyl ioyne *Anthony Munday*, an earneft traueller in this arte, and in whofe name I haue feene very excellent workes, among which furely, the moft exquifite vaine of a witty poeticall heade is fhewed in the fweete fobs of Sheepheardes and Nymphes: a worke well worthy to be viewed, and to bee efteemed as very rare Poetrie. With thefe I may place *Iohn Graunge*, **Knyght**, *VVylmott*, *Darrell*, **F. C.** F. K. G. B. and many other, whofe names come not nowe to my remembraunce.

This place haue I purpofely referued for one, who if not only, yet in my iudgement principally deferueth the tytle of the righteft Englifh Poet, that euer I read: that is, the Author of the Sheepeheardes Kalender, intituled to the woorthy Gentleman Mafter *Phillip Sydney*, whether it was Mafter *Sp.* or what rare Scholler in Pembrooke Hall foeuer, becaufe himfelf and his freendes, for what refpect I knowe not, would not reueale it, I force not greatly to fette downe: forry I am that I can not find none other with whom I might couple him in this *Catalogue*, in his rare gyft of Poetry: although one there is, though nowe long fince, ferioufly occupied in grauer ftudies, (Mafter *Gabriell Haruey*) yet, as he was once his moft fpecial freende and fellow Poet, fo becaufe he hath taken fuch paynes, not onely in his Latin Poetry (for which he enioyed great commendations of the beft both in iudgment and dignity in thys Realme) but alfo to reforme our Englifh verfe, and to beautify the fame with **braue** deuifes, of which **I** thinke the cheefe **lye** hidde in hatefull obfcurity: therefore wyll I aduenture to **fette them together, as** two of the rareft witts, **and** learnedft **mafters of** Poetrie in England. Whofe **worthy and notable** fkyl **in** this **faculty, I would wyfh if their** high dignities and **ferious** bufineffes would **permit, they would** ftyll **graunt to bee a** furtheraunce to **that reformed kinde of Poetry, which** Mafter *Haruey* did once beginne to ratify: **and furely in** mine opinion, **if hee** had chofen fome grauer **matter, and** handled **but with** halfe **that** fkyll, which I knowe **he could haue** doone, and **not** powred it foorth at a **venture, as a** thinge betweene ieft **and** earneft, it had **taken greater** effect **then** it did.

As for the other Gentleman, **if it would** pleafe him or hys freendes to let thofe excellent *Poemes*, whereof I know he hath **plenty, come** abroad, as **his** Dreames, his Legends, his **Court of** *Cupid*, his Englifh **Poet with** other: he fhoulde not onely ftay the rude pens **of my felfe and others, but** alfo fatiffye the thirfty defires of many which **defire** nothing **more,** then to **fee** more of hys rare inuentions. **If I** ioyne **to Mafter** *Haruey* **hys two** Brethren, I am affured, though **they be both** bufied with great and waighty callinges (the one a godly **and** learned Diuine, the other a famous and fkylfull Phifition) **yet if they** lyfted **to** fette to their helping **handes to** Poetry, they would **as** much beautify **and adorne it as any** others.

If I let paffe the vncountable **rabble of** ryming Ballet makers and compylers of fenceleffe fonets, **who** be moft **bufy, to ftuffe euery** ftall **full** of groffe deuifes and vn-**learned** Pamphlets: **I truft I** fhall **with the** beft fort be **held** excufed. **'Nor** though many fuch can frame **an** Alehoufe **fong of fiue of** fixe fcore verfes, hobbling vppon **fome** tune **of a Northen** Tygge, or Robyn hoode, or **La** lubber etc. **And** perhappes **o**bferue iuft **number** of fillables, eyght in one line, fixe **in** an other, **and** there withall an A to make a iercke in the ende: yet if thefe

Englifh Poetrie. 37

might be accounted Poets (as it is fayde fome of them make meanes to be promoted to ye Lawrell) furely we fhall fhortly haue whole fwarmes of Poets: and euery one that can frame a Booke in Ryme, though for want of matter, it be but in commendations of Copper nofes or Bottle Ale, wyll catch at the Garlande due to Poets: whofe potticall poeticall (I fhould fay) heades, I would wyfhe, at their worfhipfull comencements might in fteede of Lawrell, be gorgioufly garnifhed with fayre greene Barley, in token of their good affection to our Englifhe Malt. One fpeaketh thus homely of them, with whofe words I wyll content my felfe for thys time, becaufe I woulde not bee too broade wyth them in myne owne fpeeche.

' In regarde (he meaneth of the learned framing the newe Poets workes which writt the Sheepheardes Calender.) I fcorne and fpue out the rakehelly rout of our ragged Rymers, (for fo themfelues vfe to hunt the Letter) which without learning boafte, without iudgment iangle, without reafon rage and fume, as if fome inftinct of poeticall fpyrite had newlie rauifhed them, aboue the meaneffe of common capacity. And beeing in the midft of all their brauery, fuddainly for want of matter or of Ryme, or hauing forgotten their former conceyt, they feeme to be fo payned and trauelled in theyr remembraunce, as it were a woman in Chyldbyrth, or as that fame *Pythia* when the traunce came vpon her. *Os rabidum fera corda domans etc.* ' E K

Hus farre foorth haue I aduentured to fette downe parte of my fimple iudgement concerning thofe Poets, with whom for the moft part I haue beene acquainted through myne owne reading: which though it may

seeme something impertinent to the tytle of my Booke, yet I trust the courteous Readers wyll pardon me, considering that poetry is not of that grounde and antiquity in our English tongue, but that speaking thereof only as it is English, would seeme like vnto the drawing of ones pycture without a heade.

Nowe therefore by your gentle patience, wyll I wyth like breuity make tryall, what I can say concerning our Englishe Poetry, first in the matter thereof, then in the forme, that is, the manner of our verse: yet so as I must euermore haue recourse to those times and wryters, whereon the English poetry taketh as it were the discent and proprietye.

English Poetry therefore beeing confidered according to common custome and auncient vse, is, where any worke is learnedly compiled in meafurable speeche, and framed in wordes contayning number or proportion of iust syllables, delighting the readers or hearers as well by the apt and decent framing of wordes in equall refemblance of quantity, commonly called verse, as by the skyllfull handling of the matter whereof it is intreated. I spake somewhat of the beginning of thys meafuring of wordes in iust number, taken out of *Plato*: and indeede the regarde of true quantity in Letters and syllables, seemeth not to haue been much vrged before the time of *Homer* in Greece, as *Aristotle* witnesseth.

The matters whereof verses were first made, were eyther exhortations to vertue, dehortations from vice, or the prayses of some laudable thing. From thence they beganne to vse them in exercises of immitating some vertuous and wife man at their feastes: where as some one shoulde be appointed to reprefent an other mans person of high estimation, and he sang fine ditties and wittie sentences, tunably to their Musick notes. Of thys sprang the first kinde of Comedyes, when they beganne to bring into these exercises, more persons then one, whose speeches were deuised Dyalogue wise, in aunswering one another. And of such like exercises, or as some wyll needes haue it, long before the other, began the first Tragedies, and were so called of τραγος, becaufe the Actor when he began to play his part, slewe and offered a Goate to their Goddeffe: but Commedies tooke their name of κομάζειν και ᾄδειν *comessatum ire*, to goe a feasting, becaufe they vfed to goe in proceffion with their fport about the Citties and Villages, mingling much pleafaunt myrth wyth theyr graue Religion, and feafting cheerefully together wyth as great ioy as might be deuifed. But not long after (as one delight draweth another) they began to inuent new persons and newe matters for their Comedies, fuch as the deuifers thought meeteft to pleafe the peoples vaine: And from thefe, they beganne to prefent in fhapes of men, the natures of vertues and vices, and affections and quallities incident to men, as Iuftice, Temperance, Pouerty, Wrathe, Vengeaunce, Sloth, Valiantnes, and fuch like, as may appeare by the auncient workes of *Ariftophanes*. There grewe at laft to be a greater diuerfitye betweene Tragedy wryters and Comedy wryters, the one expreffing onely forrow-full and lamentable Hyftories, bringing in the perfons of Gods and Goddeffes, Kynges and Queenes, and great ftates, whofe parts were cheefely to expreffe moft miferable calamities and dreadfull chaunces, which increafed worfe and worfe, tyll they came to the moft wofull plight that might be deuifed.

The Comedies on the other fide, were directed to a contrary ende, which beginning doubtfully, drewe to fome trouble or turmoyle, and by fome lucky chaunce alwayes ended to the ioy and appeafement of all parties. Thys diftinction grewe as fome holde opinion, by immitation of the workes of *Homer*: for out of his *Iliads*, the Tragedy wryters founde dreadfull euents, whereon to frame their matters, and the other out of hys *Odyffea* tooke arguments of delight, and pleafant ending after dangerous and troublefome doubtes. So that, though there be many fortes of poeticall wrytings, and Poetry is not debarred from any matter, which may be expreffed by penne or fpeeche, yet for the better vnderftanding, and breefer method of thys difcourfe, I may comprehende the fame in three fortes, which are Comicall, Tragicall, Hiftori[c]all. Vnder the firft, may be contained all fuch *Epigrammes, Elegies* and delectable ditties, which Poets haue deuifed refpecting onely the delight thereof: in the feconde, all dolefull complaynts, lamentable chaunces, and what foeuer is poetically expreffed in forrow and heauines. In the third, we may comprife, the refte of all fuch matters, which is indifferent betweene the other two, doo commonly occupy the pennes of Poets: fuch, are the poeticall compyling of Chronicles, the freendly greetings betweene freendes, and very many fortes befides, which for the better diftinction may be referred to one of thefe three kindes of Poetry. But once againe, leaft my difcourfe runne too farre awry, wyll I buckle my felfe more neerer to Englifh Poetry: the vfe wherof, becaufe it is nothing different from any other, I thinke beft to confirme by the teftimony of *Horace*, a man worthy to beare authority in this matter: whofe very opinion is this, that the perfect perfection of poetrie is this, to mingle delight with profitt in fuch wyfe, that a Reader might by his reading be pertaker of bothe, which though I touched in the beginning, yet I thought good to alledge in this place for more confirmation thereof fome of hys owne wordes. In his treatife *de arte Poetica*, thus hee fayth.

Aut prodeffe volunt aut delectare **poetæ**,
Aut *fimul et incunda* **et** *idonea dicere vitæ.*

As much to faie: All Poets defire either by their works to profitt or delight men, or els to ioyne both profitable and pleafant leffons together for the inftruction of life.

And again

*Omne **tulit** punctum qui miscuit **vtile** dulci,*
Lectorum delectando pariterque mouendo.

That is, He miffeth nothing of his marke which ioyneth profitt with delight, as well delighting his Readers, as profiting them with counfell. And that whole Epistle which hee wryt of his Arte of Poetrie, among all the parts thereof, runneth cheefelie vppon this, that whether the argument which the Poet handleth, be of thinges doone, or fained inuentions, yet that they fhould beare fuch an Image of trueth, that as they delight they may likewife profit. For thefe are his wordes. *Ficta voluptatis caufa fint proxima veris.* Let thinges that are faigned for pleafures fake, haue a neere refemblance of ye truth. This precept may you perceiue to bee moft duelie obferued of *Chawcer:* for who could with more delight, prefcribe fuch wholfome counfaile and fage aduife, where he feemeth onelie to refpect the profitte of his leffons and inftructions? or who coulde with greater wifedome, or more pithie fkill, vnfold fuch pleafant and delightfome matters of mirth, as though they refpected nothing, but the telling of a merry tale? fo that this is the very grounde of right poetrie, to giue profitable counfaile, yet fo as it muft be mingled with delight. For among all the auncient works of poetrie, though the moft of them incline much to that part of delighting men with pleafant matters of fmall importaunce, yet euen in the vaineft trifles among them, there is not forgotten fome profitable counfaile, which a man may learne, either by flatte precepts which therein are prefcribed, or by loathing fuch vile vices, the enormities whereof they largelie difcouer. For furelie, I am of this opinion, that the wantoneft Poets of all, in their moft laciuious workes wherein they bufied themfelues, fought rather by that meanes to withdraw mens mindes (efpeciallie the beft natures) from fuch foule vices, then to allure them to imbrace fuch beaftly follies as they detected.

Horace speaking **of** the generall ducties of Poets, fayth, *Os tenerum pueri balbumque poeta fugitat*, and manie more wordes concerning the **profitte** to be hadde out of Poets, which becaufe **I** haue **fome** of them comprifed into an Englifh tranflation of that learned and famous knight, **Sir** *Thomas Elyot*, **I** wyll **fet** downe his wordes.

> **The Poet** fafhioneth by fome pleafant meane,
> The fpeeche of children ftable and vnfure:
> Gulling their eares from wordes and thinges vncleane,
> Giuing to them precepts that are pure:
> Rebuking enuy and wrath if it dure:
> Thinges well donne he can by example commend,
> To needy and ficke he doth alfo his **cure**
> **To** recomfort if ought he can amende.

And manie other like wordes are in that place **of** *Horace* to like effect. Therefore poetrie, as it is of it felfe, without abufe is not onely not vnprofitable to the liues and ftudies of menne, **but** wonderfull commendable and of great excellencie. **For** nothing can be more acceptable to men, or rather **to be wifhed,** then fweete allurements to vertues, and commodious caueates from vices? of which Poetrie is exceeding plentifull, powring into gentle witts, not roughly and tirannicallie, but it is were with a louing authoritie. Nowe if the ill and vndecent prouocations, whereof fome vnbridled witts take occafion by the reading of laciuious Poemes, bee obiected: fuch as are *Ouids* loue Bookes, and *Elegies*, *Tibullus*, *Catullus*, **and** *Martials* workes, with **the** Comedies for the **moft part of** *Plautus* and *Terence*: **I** thinke it eafily aunfwered. For though it may not iuftlie be denied, that thefe workes are indeede very Poetrie, yet that Poetrie in them **is** not the effentiall or formall matter or caufe of **the hurt** therein might be affirmed, **and** although that **reafon** fhould come fhort, yet this might be fufficient, that the workes themfelues doo not cor**rupt, but** the abufe **of** the vfers, who vndamaging their owne difpofitions, by reading the difcoueries of vices, refemble foolifh folke, who comming into a Garden without anie choife or circumfpection tread downe the faireft flowers, and wilfullie thruft their fingers among the nettles.

And furelie to fpeake what I verelie thinke, this is mine opinion: that one hauing fufficient fkyll, to reade and vnderftand thofe workes, and yet no ftaie of him felfe to auoyde inconueniences, which the remembraunce of vnlawfull things may ftirre vppe in his minde, he, in my iudgement, is wholy to bee reputed a laciuious difpofed perfonne, whom the recitall of fins whether it be in a good worke or a badde, or vppon what occafion foeuer, wyll not ftaie him but prouoke him further vnto them. Contrariwife, what good leffons the warie and fkylful Readers fhall picke out of the very worft of them, if they lift to take anie heede, and reade them not of an intent to bee made the worfe by them, you may fee by thefe fewe fentences, which the forefayd Sir *Thomas Elyott* gathered as he fayth at all aduentures, intreating of the like argument. Firft *Plautus* in commendations of vertue, hath fuch like wordes.

> Verely vertue doth all thinges excell,
> For if liberty, health liuing or fubftaunce,
> Our Country our parents, and children doo well,
> It hapneth by vertue: fhe doth all aduaunce,
> Vertue hath all thinges vnder gouernaunce:
> And in whom of vertue is founde great plenty,
> Any thing that is good may neuer be dainty.

Terence, in *Eunucho* hath a profitable fpeeche, in blafing foorth the fafhions of 'harlots, before the eyes of young men. Thus fayth *Parmeno*.

> In thys thing I tryumphe in myne owne conceite,
> That I haue found for all young men the way,
> Howe they of Harlots fhall know the deceite,
> Their witts and manners: that thereby they may
> Them perpetuallie hate, for fo much as they

Out of their owne houses be fresh and delicate,
Feeding curiously: at home all day
Lyuing beggerlie in most wretched estate.

And many more wordes of the same matter, but which may be gathered by these fewe.

Ouid, in his most wanton Bookes of loue, and the remedies thereof, hath very many pithie and wise sentences, which a heedefull Reader may marke, and chose out from ye other stuffe. This is one.

Tyme is a medicine of it shall profitt,
VVine gyuen out of tyme may be annoyaunce.
And man shall irritat vice if he prohibitt,
VVhen time is not meete vnto his vtteraunce.
Therfore if thou yet by counsayle art recuperable,
Fly thou from idlenes and euer be stable.

Martiall, a most dissolute wryter among all other, yet not without many graue and prudent speeches, as this is one worthy to be marked of these fond youthes which intangle theyr wytts in raging loue, who stepping once ouer shoes in theyr fancyes, neuer rest plunging till they be ouer head and eares in their follie.

If thou wylt eschewe bitter aduenture,
And auoyde the annoyance of a pensifull hart,
Set in no one person all wholly thy pleasure,
The lesse maist thou ioy, but the lesse shalt thou smart.

These are but fewe gathered out by happe, yet sufficient to shewe that the wise and circumspect Readers may finde very many profitable lessons, dispersed in these workes, neither take any harme by reading such Poemes, but good, if they wil themselues. Neuertheles, I would not be thought to hold opinion, that the reading of them is so tollerable, as that there neede no respect to be had in making choyse of readers or hearers: for if they be prohibited from the tender and vnconstant wits of children and young mindes, I thinke it not without great reason: neyther am I of that deuilish opinion, of which some there are, and haue beene in England, who hauing charge of youth to instruct them in learning, haue especially made choyse of such vnchildish stuffe, to reade vnto young Schollers, as it shoulde seeme of some filthy purpose, wylfully to corrupt theyr tender mindes, and prepare them the more ready for theyr loathsome dyetts.

For as it is sayd of that impudent worke of *Luciane*, a man were better to reade none of it then all of it, so thinke I that these workes are rather to be kept altogether from children, then they should haue free liberty to reade them, before they be meete either of their owne discretion or by heedefull instruction, to make choyse of the good from the badde. As for our Englishe Poetrie, I know no such perilous peeces (except a fewe balde ditties made ouer the Beere potts, which are nothing lesse then Poetry) which anie man may vse and reade without damage or daunger: which indeede is lesse to be meruailed at among vs, then among the olde Latines and Greekes, considering that Christianity may be a staie to such illecibrous workes and inuentions, as among them (for their Arte sake) myght obtaine passage.

Nowe will I speake somewhat, of that princelie part of Poetrie, wherein are displaied the noble actes and valiant exploits of puissaunt Captaines, expert souldiers, wise men, with the famous reportes of auncient times, such as are the Heroycall workes of *Homer* in Greeke, and the heauenly verse of *Virgils Æneidos* in Latine: which workes, comprehending as it were the summe and ground of all Poetrie, are verelie and incomparably the best of all other. To these, though wee haue no English worke aunswerable, in respect of the glorious ornaments of gallant handling: yet our auncient Chroniclers and reporters of our Countrey affayres, come most neere them: and no doubt, if such regarde of our English speeche, and curious handling of our verse, had beene long since thought vppon, and from time to time been pollished and bettered by men of learning, iudgement, and authority, it would ere this, haue matched them in all respects. A manifest example thereof, may bee **the** great **good** grace and sweete vayne, which Eloquence hath attained in our speeche, because it hath had the helpe of such **rare and** singuler wits, as from time to time myght still adde some amendment **to the** same. Among whom **I thinke** there is none **that** will gainsay, **but** Master *Iohn Lilly* **hath deserued** moste high commendations, as he **which** hath stept one steppe further therein then any **either** before **or** since **he** first began the wyttie discourse of his *Euphues*. Whose **workes,** surely in respecte of his singuler eloquence and braue composition of apt words and sentences, let the learned examine and make tryall thereof thorough all the partes **of** Rethoricke, in fitte phrases, in pithy sentences, in gallan**t tropes,** in flowing speeche, in plaine sence, and surely in my iudgment, I thinke he wyll yeelde him that verdict, which *Quintilian* giueth of bothe **the** best **Orators** *Demosthenes* **and** *Tully*, that from **the one, nothing** may be taken away, to the other, nothing **may be** added. But a more neerer example to prooue **my former** assertion true (I **meane** ye meetnesse **of our** speeche to receiue the best forme of Poetry) may bee taken by conference **of that** famous translation of Master D. *Phaer* with the coppie it selfe, who soeuer pleafe with courteous iudgement but **a** little to compare and marke them both together : and **weigh with** himselfe, whether the English tongue might **by little and** little be brought to the verye maiesty of a ryght Heroicall verse. First you may marke, how *Virgill* alwayes fitteth his matter in hande with wordes agree**able vnto the same affection,** which he expresseth, as in hys Tragicall **exclamations, what** pathe[ti]call speeches he frameth? **in his** comfortable consolations, howe smoothely hys verse runnes? in his dreadfull battayles, **and** dreery byckerments of warres, howe bygge and boystrous his wordes sound? and the like notes in all partes **of** his work**e** may be obserued. Which excellent

English Poetrie.   47

grace and comely kind of choyfe, if the tranflatour hath not hitte very neere in our courfe Englifh phrafe iudge vprightly: wee wyll conferre fome of the places, not picked out for the purpofe, but fuch as I tooke turning ouer the Booke at randon. When the Troyans were fo toft about in tempeftious wether, caufed by *Æolus* at *Iunoes* requeft, and driuen vpon the coafte of *Affrick* with a very neere fcape of their liues: *Æneas* after hee had gone a land and kylled plenty of victuals for his company of Souldiours, hee deuided the fame among them, and thus louinglie and fweetely he comforted them. *Æn. Lib. i.*

> *et dictis mœrentia pectora* **mulcet**
> *O focii (neque ignari fumus* **ante malorum)**
> *O pafsi grauiora: dabit deus* **his quoque finem** *.*
> *Vos et fcyllæam rabiem,* **penitufque** *fonantes,*
> *Accestis fcopulos: vos et* **cyclopea faxa**
> *Experti, reuocate* **animos, mæftumque** *timorem*
> *Mittite, forfan* **et hæc olim meminiffe** *iuuabit.*
> *Per varios cafus, per tot difcrimina* **rerum**
> *Tendimus in Latium: fedes vbi fata* **quietas**
> *Ostendunt, illic fas regna refurgere troiæ.*
> **Durate,** *et vofmet rebus feruate fecundis.*
> **Talia voce** *refert, curifque ingentibus æger*
> **Spem** *vultu fimulat, premit altum corde* **dolorem.**

Tranflated thus.

And then to cheere their heauy harts with thefe words he
   him bent.
O Mates (quoth he) that many a woe haue bidden and
   borne ere thys,
Worfe haue we feene, and this alfo fhall end when Gods
   wyll is.
Through *Sylla* rage (ye wott) and through the roaring
   rocks we paft,
Though *Cyclops* fhore was full of feare, yet came we
   through at laft.

Plucke vppe your harts, and driue from thence both
  feare and care away.
To thinke on this may pleafure be perhapps another day.
By paynes and many a daunger fore, by fundry chaunce
  we wend,
To come to *Italy*, where we truft to find our refting ende:
And where the deftnyes haue decreed *Troyes* Kingdome
  eft to ryfe
Be bold and harden now your harts, take eafe while eafe
  applies
Thus fpake he tho, but in his hart huge cares had him
  oppreft,
Diffembling hope with outward eyes full heauy was his
  breft.

Againe, marke the wounding of *Dido* in loue with
Æneas, with howe choyfe wordes it is pithily defcribed,
both by the Poet and the tranflator in the beginning
of the fourth booke.

  At Regina graui iam dudum faucia cura
    Volnus alit venis, et cæco carpitur igni, etc.

By this time perced fatte the Queene fo fore with loues
  defire,
Her wound in euery vayne fhe feedes, fhe fryes in
  fecrete fire.
The manhood of the man full oft, full oft his famous lyne
She doth reuolue, and from her thought his face cannot
  vntwyne.
His countnaunce deepe fhe drawes and fixed faft fhe
  beares in breft,
His words alfo, nor to her carefull hart can come no reft.

And in many places of the fourth booke is the fame matter fo gallantly profecuted in fweete wordes, as in mine
opinion the coppy it felfe goeth no whit beyond it.
  Compare them likewife in the woefull and lamentable

English Poetrie.

cryes of the Queene for the departure of *Æneas*, towards the ende of that Booke.

Terque quaterque manu pectus **percussa** *decorum*
Fauentisque abscissa **comas, proh** *Iupiter,* **ibit?**
Hic ait, et nostris inluserit aduena **Regnis?** *etc.*

Three times **her hands she bet, and** three times strake her comely brest,
Her golden **hayre** she **tare and frantiklike** with moode opprest,
She **cryde, O** *Iupiter*, O God, **quoth she, and** shall a goe?
Indeede? and shall a flowte **me thus within my king-dome so?**
Shall not mine Armies out, and all my people **them pursue?**
Shall they **not** spoyle their shyps and burne **them vp with** vengance **due?**
Out people, **out** vppon them, follow fast with **fires and** flames,
Set fayles **aloft,** make out with oares, in ships, in boates, in frames.
What speake **I?** or where am **I?** what furies me **doo** thus inchaunt?
O *Dydo*, wofull wretch, **now** destnyes fell thy head dooth haunt.

And a little after preparing **to kyll her** owne selfe.

But *Dydo* quaking fierce with **frantike** moode and griesly hewe.
With trembling spotted cheekes, her huge attempting **to** persue.
Besides her **selfe for** rage, and towards **death** with visage wanne,
Her eyes **about she** rolde, as redde as **blood they** looked than.

D

At laſt ready to fall vppon *Æneas* ſworde.

O happy (welaway) and ouer happy had I beene,
If neuer Troian ſhyps (ahlas) my Country ſhore had ſeene.
Thus ſayd ſhe wryde her head, and vnreuenged muſt we die?
But let vs boldly die (quoth ſhee) thus, thus to death I ply.

Nowe likewiſe for the braue warlike phraſe and bygge ſounding kynd of thundring ſpeeche, in the hotte ſkyrmyſhes of battels, you may confer them in any of the laſt fiue Bookes: for examples ſake, thys is one about the ninth Booke.

> *Et clamor* **totis per propugnacula muris,**
> *Intendunt acries arcus, amentaque torquent.*
> *Sternitur* **omne** *ſolum telis, tum ſcuta cauæque*
> *Dant ſonitum flictu galeæ: pugna asper ſurgit?* etc.

A clamarous noyſe vpmounts on fortreſſe tops and bulwarks towres,
They ſtrike, they bend their bowes, they whirle from ſtrings ſharp ſhoting ſhowres.
All ſtreetes with tooles are ſtrowed, than helmets, ſkulles, with battrings marrd.
And ſhieldes diſhyuering cracke, vpriſeth roughneſſe byckring hard
Looke how the tempeſt ſtorme when wind out wraſtling blowes at ſouth,
Raine ratling beates the grownde, or clowdes of haile from Winters mouth,
Downe daſhyng headlong driues, when God from ſkyes with grieſly ſteuen,
His watry ſhowres outwrings, and whirlwind clowdes downe breakes from heauen.

And ſo foorth much more of the like effect.

Onely one **comparifon** more **will I** defire you to marke at your leyfures, **which** may **ferue** for all the reft, that is, **the** defcription of Fame, **as it** is in the 4. booke, towardes the end, of which it followeth thus.

Monstrum horrendum ingens **cui quot** *funt corpore plumæ* **Tot** *vigilos oculi* **etc.**

Monfter gaftly great, **for** euery plume her carkaffe beares,
Like number lcaring **eyes fhe** hath, like number harkning **eares,**
Like number tongues, and mouthes **fhe** wagges, a wondrous **thing** to fpeake,
At **midnight** foorth fhee flyes, **and vnder** fhade her found dooth fqueake.
All night **fhe** wakes, nor flumber fweete **doth take nor neuer** fleepes.
By dayes **on houfes** tops **fhee fits or** gates of **Townes** fhe keepes.
On watching Towres **fhe** clymbes, and **Cities great fhe makes agaft,**
Both **trueth and** falfhood forth fhe telles, and **lyes** abroade **doth** caft.

But **what neede** I to repeate any more places? there is not one Booke among **the** twelue, which wyll **not** yeelde you moft excellent **pleafure** in **conferring** the tranflation **with the** Coppie, **and marking the** gallant **grace** which **our Englifhe fpeeche affoordeth.** And in trueth **the** like **comparifons, may you choofe** out through the whole **tranflations of the** *Metamorphofis* by Mafter *Golding* who (confidering both **their** Coppyes) hath equally deferued commendations **for the** beautifying **of the** Englifh **fpeeche.** It would be tedious to ftay to rehearfe **any** places **out** of him **nowe:** let the other fuffice **to** prooue, that the Englifh tongue lacketh neyther variety nor currantneffe of phrafe for **any** matter.

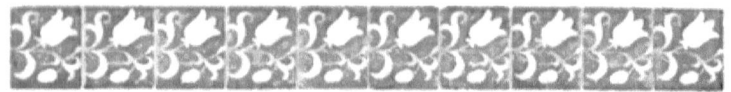

Wyll nowe speake a little of an other kinde of poetical writing, which might notwithstanding for the variablenesse of the argument therein vsually handled, bee comprehended in those kindes before declared: that is, the compyling *Eglogues*, as much to say as Goteheardes tales, because they bee commonly Dialogues or speeches framed or supposed betweene Sheepeheardes, Neteheardes, Goteheardes, or such like simple men: in which kind of writing, many haue obtained as immortall prayse and commendation, as in any other.

The cheefest of these is *Theocritus* in Greeke, next him, and almost the very same, is *Virgill* in Latin. After *Virgyl* in like sort writ *Titus Calphurnius* and *Baptista Mantuan*, wyth many other both in Latine and other languages very learnedlye. Although the matter they take in hand seemeth commonlie in appearaunce rude and homely, as the vsuall talke of simple clownes: yet doo they indeede vtter in the same much pleasaunt and profitable delight. For vnder these personnes, as it were in a cloake of simplicitie, they would eyther sette foorth the prayses of theyr freendes, without the note of flattery, or enueigh grieuously against abuses, without any token of bytternesse.

Somwhat like vnto these works, are many peeces of *Chawcer*, but yet not altogether so poeticall. But nowe yet at ye last hath England hatched vppe one Poet of this sorte, in my conscience comparable with the best in any respect: euen Master *Sp*: Author of the *Sheepeheardes Calender*, whose trauell in that peece of English Poetrie, I thinke verely is so commendable, as none of equall iudgment can yeelde him lesse prayse for **hys** excellent skyll, and skylfull excellency shewed **foorth** in the same, then they would **to** eyther *Theocritus* or *Virgill*, whom in mine opinion, if the coursenes of our speeche (I meane the **course** of custome which he woulde not infringe) **had** beene no **more let** vnto him, then **theyr pure natiue** tongues were vnto them, he would **haue (if it might** be) surpassed them. What one thing **is there in them** so worthy admiration, whereunto **we may not adioyne** some thing of **his,** of equall desert? Take *Virgil* and make some little comparison **betweene them, and** iudge **as ye** shall see **caufe.**

Virgill hath a gallant report of *Augustus* couertly compryfed in the first *Æglogue*: the like is **in him,** of her Maieslie, vnder the name of *Eliza*. *Virgill* maketh a braue coloured complaint of vnstedfast freendshyppe in the person of *Corydon*: the lyke is him in his 5 *Æglogue*. Agayne behold **the pretty Pastorall** contentions of *Virgill* in the third *Æglogue*: of him in ye eight *Eglogue*. Finally, either **in comparison with them, or** respect **of hys** owne great **learning, he may** well were **the** Garlande, and steppe before **ye best of all English Poets that** I haue seene or hearde: **for I thinke no** lesse **deserueth** (thus sayth *E, K* in hys commendations) hys **wittinesse in** deuising, **his** pithinesse in vttering, his **complaintes of loue so louely,** his discourses **of** pleasure so pleasantly, his Pastrall rudenes, his Morrall wysenesse, **his due obseruing** of *decorum* euery **where,** in personages, **in season,** in matter, in **speeche, and** generally **in all seemely** simplicity, of **handling hys** matter **and framing hys** wordes. The occasion **of his** worke is a **warning to** other young men, **who being** intangled in loue **and** youthful vanities, **may learne to** looke to themselues in time, and to auoyde inconueniences which may breede if they be **not** in time preuented. Many good Morrall lessons **are** therein contained, as the reuerence which young **men** owe **to the** aged in the second *Eglogue*: the caueate or warning to beware **a subtill** professor of freendſhippe in the fift *Eglogue*: the commendation of good Paſtors, and ſhame and diſprayſe of idle and ambitious Goteheardes in the ſeauenth, the looſe and retchleſſe lyuing of Popiſh Prelates in the ninth. The learned and ſweete complaynt of the contempt of learning vnder the name of Poetry in the tenth. There is alſo much matter vttered ſomewhat couertly, eſpecially ye abuſes of ſome whom he would not be too playne withall: in which, though it be not apparant to euery one, what hys ſpeciall meaning was, yet ſo ſkilfully is it handled, as any man may take much delight at hys learned conueyance, and picke out much good ſence in the moſt obſcureſt of it. Hys notable prayſe deſerued in euery parcell of that worke, becauſe I cannot expreſſe as I woulde and as it ſhould: I wyll ceaſe to ſpeake any more of, the rather becauſe I neuer hearde as yet any that hath reade it, which hath not with much admiration commended it. One only thing therein haue I hearde ſome curious heades call in queſtion: *viz*: the motion of ſome vnſauery loue, ſuch as in the ſixt *Eglogue* he ſeemeth to deale withall (which ſay they) is ſkant allowable to Engliſh eares, and might well haue beene left for the Italian defenders of loathſome beaſtlines, of whom perhappes he learned it: to thys obiection I haue often aunſwered and (I thinke truely) that theyr nyce opinion ouer ſhooteth the Poets meaning, who though hee in that as in other thinges, immitateth the auncient Poets, yet doth not meane, no more did they before hym, any diſordered loue, or the filthy luſt of the deuilliſh *Pederaſtice* taken in the worſe ſence, but rather to ſhewe howe the diſſolute life of young men intangled in loue of women, doo neglect the freendſhyp and league with their olde freendes and familiers. Why (ſay they) yet he ſhold gyue no occaſion of ſuſpition, nor offer to the viewe of Chriſtians, any token of ſuch filthineſſe, howe good ſoeuer hys meaning were: wherevnto I oppoſe the ſimple conceyte they haue of matters which concerne learning or wytt, wylling them to gyue

Englifh Poetrie.

Poets leaue to vfe theyr vayne as they fee good: it is their foolyfh conftruction, not hys wryting that is blameable. Wee muft prefcrybe to no wryters, (much leffe to Poets) in what forte they fhould vtter theyr conceyts. But thys wyll be better difcuffed by fome I hope of better abillity.

One other forte of Poeticall wryters remayneth yet to bee remembred, that is, The precepts of Hufbandry, learnedly compiled in Heroycall verfe. Such were the workes of *Hefiodus* in *Greeke*, and *Virgils Georgickes* in Latine. What memorable worke hath beene handled in immitation of thefe by any Englifh Poet, I know not, (faue onely one worke of M. *Tuffer*, a peece furely of great wytt and experience, and wythal very prettilye handled) And I thinke the caufe why our Poets haue not trauayled in that behalfe, is efpecially, for that there haue beene alwayes plenty of other wryters that haue handled the fame argument very largely. Among whom Mafter *Barnabe Googe*, in tranflating and enlarging the moft profitable worke of *Heresbachius*, hath deferued much commendation, as well for hys faythfull compyling and learned increafing the noble worke, as for hys wytty tranflation of a good part of the *Georgickes* of *Virgill* into Englifh verfe.

Among all the tranflations, which hath beene my fortune to fee, I could neuer yet finde that worke of the *Georgicks* wholly performed. I remember once Abraham Flemming in his conuerfion of the *Eglogues*, promifed to tranflate and publifhe it: whether he dyd or not I knowe not, but as yet I heard not of it. I my felfe wott well I beftowed fome time in it two or three yeeres fince, turning it to that fame Englifh verfe, which other fuch workes were in, though it were rudely: howe beit, I did it onely for mine owne vfe, and vppon certayne refpectes towardes a Gentleman mine efpeciall freende, to whom I was defirous to fhewe fome token of duetifull good wyll, and not minding it fhould goe farre abroade, confidering howe flenderly I ranne it ouer, yet fince then, hath one **gott** it in keeping, who as it is told me, eyther hath **or** wyll vnaduifedly publifhe it : **which** iniury though **he meanes to** doo me in myrth, yet **I hope** he wyll make **me fome** fuffycient recompence, or els **I** fhall goe **neere to** watch **hym** the like or a worfe turne.

But concerning the matter **of our** Englyfh **wryters,** lett thys fuffice : nowe fhall **ye heare** my fimple **fkyl in what I am able to fay** concerning the forme **and manner of our** Englyfhe **verfe.**

The moft vfuall and frequented kind of our Englifh **Poetry hath** alwayes **runne vpon,** and to this day **is** obferued in fuch equall number of fyllables, and likenes of wordes, that in all **places one** verfe either immediatly, **or by** mutuall **interpofition, may** be aunfwerable **to an other** both in proportion of length, **and** ending of lynes in the fame **Letters.** Which rude kinde of verfe, though (as I touched before) it rather difcrediteth our fpeeche, as borrowed from the *Barbarians,* then furnifheth the fame with any comely ornament : yet beeing **fo ingraffed by** cuftome, and frequented **by the moft parte, I may not vtterly** diffalowe it, leaft **I fhould feeme to** call **in queftion** the iudgement **of all our famous wryters, which haue** wonne **eternall prayfe by theyr** memorable **workes** compyled in that verfe.

For my part therefore, **I can be content to efteeme it as a** thing, the perfection whereof is very **commendable, yet** fo **as** wyth others **I could wyfh it were by men** of learning and **ability** bettered, **and** made **more artificiall, according to the woorthines** of our fpeeche.

The falling out of verfes together in one like founde, is commonly **called in Englifh, Ryme,** taken from the Greeke worde **P**υθμ**os,** which **furely in my** iudgment is verye abufiuelye applyed to fuch a fence : and by thys, the vnworthineffe of the thing may well appeare, in that wanting **a proper name,** wherby **to be** called, it borroweth a word farre exceeding the dignitye of it,

English Poetrie.

and not appropriate to fo rude or bafe a thing. For Ryme is properly, the iuſt proportion of a clauſe or fentence, whether it be in profe or meeter, aptly compriſed together: wherof there is both an naturall and an artificiall compoſition, in any manner or kynde of fpeeche, eyther French, Italian, Spaniſh or Engliſh: and is propper not onely to Poets, but alfo to Readers, Oratours, Pleaders, or any which are to pronounce or fpeake any thing in publike audience.

The firſt begynning of Ryme (as we nowe terme it) though it be fomewhat auncient, yet nothing famous. In Greece (they fay) one *Symias Rhodias*, becaufe he would be finguler in fomthing, wryt poetically of the Fable, contayning howe *Iupiter* beeing in ſhape of a Swanne, begatte the Egge on Leda, wherof came Caſtor, Pollux, and Helena, whereof euery verfe ended in thys Ryme, and was called therefore ὠον but thys foolyſhe attempt was fo contemned and difpyfed, that the people would neither admitte the Author nor Booke any place in memory of learning. Since that it was not hearde of, till ye time ye *Hunnes* and *Gothians* renued it agayne, and brought it into Italie. But howfoeuer or wherefoeuer it beganne, certayne it is, that in our Engliſh tongue it beareth as good grace, or rather better, then in any other: and is a faculty whereby many may and doo deferue great prayfe and commendation, though our fpeeche be capable of a farre more learned manner of verfifying, as I wyl partly declare heereafter.

There be three fpeciall notes neceſſary to be obferued in the framing of our accuſtomed Engliſh Ryme: the firſt is, that one meeter or verfe be aunfwerable to an other, in equall number of feete or fyllables, or proportionable to the tune whereby it is to be reade or meafured. The feconde, to place the words in fuch forte, as none of them be wreſted contrary to the naturall inclination or affectation of the fame, or more truely ye true quantity thereof. The thyrd, to make them fall together mutually in Ryme, that is, in wordes of like founde, but **fo** as the **wordes be** not difordered for the Rymes fake, nor the **fence** hindered. Thefe be the **moft pryncipall obferuations, which** I thinke requifite in an **Englifh verfe: for as for the** other ornaments which belong **thereto, they be** more properly belonging **to** the feuerall gyfts **of** fkylfull Poets, then common notes to be prefcribed **by me:** but fomewhat perhaps I fhall **haue** occafion **to fpeake heereafter.**

Of the kyndes **of** Englifh verfes which **differ in number of** fyllables, there **are** almoft infinite: which **euery way** alter according **to** hys fancy, **or** to the meafure of **that meeter, wherein** it pleafeth hym to frame hys **ditty.** Of the beft and moft frequented I wyll **rehearfe fome.** The longeft verfe in length, which I haue feene vfed in Englifh confifteth of fix-**teene fyllables, eache** two **verfes ryming** together, thus.

Wher vertue **wants and vice** abounds, **there wealth is but** a bayted **hooke,**
To make men swallow **down their** bane, **before** on danger deepe they looke.

Thys kynde **is not very much vfed at** length thus, but is commonly deuided, **eche verfe into** two, whereof eche fhal containe **eyght** fyllables, and ryme croffe wyfe, **the** firft to the **thyrd, and** the fecond **to the** fourth, **in** this manner.

   Great wealth is but a bayted hooke.
   VVhere vertue wants, and vice aboundes:
   VVhich men deuoure before they looke,
   So them in daungers deepe it drownes.

An other kynd next in length **to thys, is,** where eche verfe hath fourteene fyllables, **which** is the moft ac-cuftomed **of all** other, and efpecially vfed of all the tranflatours of the Latine Poets for the moft part thus.

My mind with **furye fierce** inflamde **of late I** know not howe,
Doth burne Parnaffus **hyll to** fee, adornd wyth Lawrell bowe.

Which may likewyfe and fo it often is deuyded, eche

verſe into two, to [the?] firſt hauing **eyght** ſillables, **the
ſecond** ſixe, wherof the two ſixes ſhall alwayes ryme,
and ſometimes the eyghtes, ſometimes **not**, according
to the wyll of the maker.

> My minde with furye fierce inflamde,
>   Of late I knowe not howe:
> Doth burne *Pernaſſus* hyll to ſee,
>   Adornd wyth Lawrell bowe.

There are nowe wythin this compaſſe, as many ſortes
of **verſes as** may be deuiſed **differences of numbers**:
wherof ſome conſiſt of **equall proportions**, ſome of long
and **ſhort** together, ſome **of many rymes** in one ſtaffe
(as they call it) ſome of croſſe **ryme**, ſome of counter
ryme, ſome ryming wyth one worde farre diſtant from
another, ſome ryming euery thyrd or fourth word, and
ſo likewyſe all manner of dytties applyable to euery
tune that may be ſung or ſayd, diſtinct from profe or
continued ſpeeche. To auoyde therefore tedioufneſſe
and confuſion, I wyll repeate onely the **different ſortes
of verſes out of the** *Sheepeheardes Calender*, **which**
may well ſerue to beare authoritie in thys matter.

There **are in** that **worke** twelue or thirteene **ſundry
forts of verſes, which differ** eyther **in length, or ryme,
of** deſtinction **of the ſtaues:** but **of them which differ
in** length or number of **fillables** not paſt **ſixe** or ſeauen.
The firſt of **them** is of **tenne** fillables, **or** rather fiue
feete in one **verſe,** thus,

> A Sheepheards boy **no better doo** him call,
> When Winters waſtfull ſpight **was** almoſt ſpent.

This verſe he vſeth commonly **in** hys ſweete com-
playntes, **and** mornefull ditties, as very agreeable to
ſuch affections.

The ſecond **ſort hath naturally** but nyne ſyllables,
and is a more rough or clowniſh manner of verſe, vſed
moſt commonly **of** him **if you mark** him **in hys**

fatyricall reprehenfions, and his Sheepeheardes homelyeſt talke, fuch as the fecond *Æglogue* is.

Ah for pitty wyll rancke Winters rage,
Thefe bytter blaſts neuer gynne to affwage.

The number of nine fillables in thys verfe is very often altered, and fo it may without any difgrace to the fame, efpecially where the fpeeche fhould be moſt clownifh and fimple, which is much obferued of hym.

The third kynd is a pretty rounde verfe, running currantly together, commonly feauen fillables or fometime eyght in one verfe, as many in the next, both ryming together: euery two hauing one the like verfe after them, but of rounder wordes, and two of them likewyfe ryming mutually. That verfe expreffeth notably, light and youthfull talke, fuch as is the thyrde *Æglogue* betweene two Sheepheardes boys concerning loue.

> *Thomalin* why fitten we fo
> As weren ouerwent with woe
> Vpon fo fayre a morrowe?
> The ioyous time now nigheth faſt
> That wyll allay this bitter blaſt
> And flake the Winter forrow.

The fourth fort containeth in eche ſtaffe manie vnequall verfes, but moſt fweetelie falling together: which the Poet calleth the tune of the waters fall. Therein is his fong In prayfe of *Eliza*.

> Ye daintie Nymphes which in this bleffed brooke
>   doo bathe your breſt,
> Forfake your watrie bowres and hether looke,
>   at my requeſt.
> And eke yée Virgins that on *Parnafs* dwell,
> Whence floweth *Helicon* the learned Well,
>   helpe me to blaze
>   her woorthy praife
> That in her fex doth all excell. etc.

Englifh Poetrie.

The fift, is a deuided verfe of twelue fillables into two verfes, whereof I fpake before, and feemeth moft meete for ye handling of a Morrall matter, fuch as is the praife of good Paftors, and the difpraife of ill in the feauenth *Æglogue*.

The fixt kinde, is called a round, beeing mutuallie fung betweene two: one fingeth one verfe, the other the next, eche rymeth with himfelfe.

> Per. It fell vppon a holie eue
> Wyl. Hey ho holliday
> Per. When holie fathers wont to fhrieue,
> Wyl. Thus ginneth our Rondelay. etc.

The feauenth forte is a verie tragicall mournefull meafure, wherein he bewayleth the death of fome freend vnder the perfon of *Dydo*.

> Vp then *Melpomene* the mournfulft Mufe of nyne,
> fuch caufe of mourning neuer hadft afore:
> Vp griefly ghoftes, and vp my mournfull ryme:
> matter of myrth now fhalt thou haue no more.
> *Dydo* my deere alas is dead,
> Dead and lyeth wrapt in leade:
> O heauie hearfe
> Let ftreaming teares be powred out in ftore
> O carefull vearfe.

Thefe fortes of verfes for breuities fake haue I chofen foorth of him, whereby I fhall auoide the tedious rehearfall of all the kindes which are vfed: which I thinke would haue beene vnpoffible, feeing they may be altered to as manie formes as the Poets pleafe: neither is there anie tune or ftroke which may be fung or plaide on inftruments, which hath not fome poetical ditties framed according to the numbers thereof: fome to Rogero, fome to Trenchmore, to downe right Squire, to Galliardes, to Pauines, to Iygges, to Brawles, to all manner of tunes which euerie Fidler knowes better then my felfe, and therefore I will let them paffe.

Againe, the diuersities of the **staues** (which are the number **of** verses **contained with the** diuisions or **partitions of a** ditty) **doo often times make** great differences in **these verses.** As when **one staffe** containeth but two **verses, or (if they bee** deuided) foure: **the** first or the first couple hauing twelue **sillables, the other** fourteene, which versifyers call **Powlters measure,** becaufe so they tall[i]e their wares by **dozens.** Also, **when one** staffe **hath** manie **verses,** whereof **eche one** rimeth **to** the next, **or** mutuallie crosse, **or distant by three, or by foure, or** ended contrarye to the beginning, **and a hundred** sortes, whereof **to** shewe seuerall examples, **would bee too** troublesome: nowe for the second point.

The naturall **course of most** English verses seemeth **to run vppon the olde** Iambicke stroake, **and I may well** thinke **by all likelihoode,** it had the beginning **thereof. For if you marke the** right **quantitie of our** vsuall **verses, ye shall** perceiue them **to** containe **in sound ye very** propertie of **Iambick** feete, as thus.

˘ — ˘ — ˘ — ˘ — ˘ — ˘ — ˘ —
I that my slender oaten pipe in verse was wont to sounde:

For transpose anie **of** those feete **in** pronouncing, **and** make short either **the** two, foure, sixe, eight, tenne, twelue sillable, **and it** will (doo what you can) fall **out** very absurdly.

Againe, though our wordes can not well bee forced **to** abyde the touch **of** *Position* and other rules of *Prosodia*, **yet** is there **such a** naturall **force or** quantity in **eche worde, that** it will not abide anie place but one, **without some foule** disgrace: as **for** example try anie **verse, as thys,**

˘ — ˘ — ˘ — ˘ — ˘ — ˘ — ˘ —
Of shapes transformde to bodies **strange I** purpose to intreate.
Make the first sillable long, **or the** third, or the fift and **so foorth: or** contrariwise **make the** other sillables to **admitte the** shortnesse **of one of** them places, and see

what a wonderfull defacing it wil be to the wordes, as thus.

— ᴗ — ᴗ — ᴗ — ᴗ — ᴗ — ᴗ — ᴗ
Of ſtrange bodies tranſformd to ſhapes purpoſe I to intreat.

So that this is one eſpeciall thing to be taken heede of in making a good Engliſh verſe, that by diſplacing no worde bee wreſted againſt his naturall propriety, where-vnto you ſhal perceyue eche worde to be affected, and may eaſilie diſcerne it in wordes of two ſillables or aboue, though ſome there be of indifferencie, that wyll ſtand in any place. Againe, in chouching the whole ſentence, the like regarde is to be had, that wee exceede not too boldly in placing the verbe out of his order, and too farre behinde the nowne: which the neceſſitie of Ryme may oftentimes vrge. For though it be tollerable in a verſe to ſette wordes ſo extraordinarily as other ſpeeche will not admitt, yet heede is to be taken, leaſt by too much affecting that manner, we make both the verſe vnpleaſant and the ſence obſcure. And ſure it is a wonder to ſee the folly of manie in this reſpect, that vſe not onely too much of thys ouerthwart placing, or rather diſplacing of wordes, in theyr Poemes and verſes, but alſo in theyr proſe or continued writings: where they thinke to rolle moſt ſmoothlie, and flow moſt eloquently, there by this means, come foorth theyr ſentences dragging at one Authors tayle as they were tyde together with poynts, where often you ſhall tarrie (ſcratching your heade) a good ſpace before you ſhall heare hys principall verbe or ſpeciall word, leaſte hys ſinging grace, which in his ſentence is contained ſhould be leſſe, and his ſpeeche ſeeme nothing poeticall.

The thyrd obſeruation is, the Ryme or like ending of verſes: which though it is of leaſt importance, yet hath won ſuch credite among vs, that of all other it is moſt regarded of the greateſt part of Readers. And ſurely as I am perſwaded, the regarde of wryters to this, hath beene the greateſt decay of that good order of verſifying, which might ere this haue beene eſtabliſhed in our speeche. In my iudgment, if there be any ornament in the same, it is rather to be attributed to the plentifull fulnesse of our speeche, which can affoorde ryming words sufficient for the handling of any matter, then to the thing it selfe for any beautifying it bringeth to a worke: which might bee adorned with farre more excellent collours then ryming is. Notwithstanding I cannot but yeelde vnto it (as custome requireth) the deserued prayses, especially where it is with good iudgement ordered. And I thinke them right worthy of admiration, for their readines and plenty of wytt and capacity, who can with facility intreate at large, and as we call it *extempore*, in good and sencible ryme, vppon some vnacquainted matter.

The ready skyll of framing anie thing in verse, besides the naturall promptnesse which many haue therevnto, is much helped by Arte, and exercise of the memory: for as I remember, I reade once among *Gaskoynes* workes, a little instruction to versifying, where is prescribed as I thinke thys courfe of learning to versifye in Ryme.

When ye haue one verse well setled, and decently ordered which you may dispose at your pleasure, to ende it with what word you wyll: then what soeuer the word is, you may speedilie runne ouer the other wordes which are aunswerable therevnto, (for more readines through all the letters Alphabetically) whereof you may choose that which wyll best fitte the sence of your matter in that place: as for example: if your last worde ende in Booke, you may straightwayes in your minde runne them ouer thus. Brooke, Cooke, crooke, hooke, looke, nooke, pooke, rooke, forsooke, tooke, awooke etc. Nowe it is twenty to one, but alwayes one of these shall iumpe with your former worde and matter in good sence. If not, then alter the first.

And indeede I thinke, that next to the Arte of memory, thys is the readyest way to attaine to the faculty of ryming well Extempore, especially if it be helped with thus much paynes. Gather together all manner of wordes efpecially *Monafillables*, and place them Alphabetically in fome note, and either haue them meetely perfectly by hart (which is no verye labourfome matter) or but looke them dilligently ouer at fome time, practifing to ryme indifferent often, whereby I am perfwaded it wil foone be learned, fo as the party haue withall any reafonable gyft of knowledge and learning, whereby hee want not bothe matter and wordes altogether.

What the other circumftaunces of Ryming are, as what wordes may tollerably be placed in Ryme, and what not: what words doo beft become a Ryme, and what not, how many fortes of Ryme there is: and fuch like I wyll not ftay nowe to intreate. There be many more obferuations and notes to be prefcribed, to the exacte knowledge of verfifying, which I truft wilbe better and larger laide forth by others, to whom I deferre manie confiderations in this treatife: hoping that fome of greater fkill will fhortlie handle this matter in better forte.

Nowe the fundry kindes of rare deuifes, and pretty inuentions which come from ye fine poeticall vaine of manie in ftrange and vnacuftomed manner, if I could report them, it were worthie my trauell: fuch are the turning of verfes: the infolding of wordes: the fine repititions: the clarklie conueying of contraries, and manie fuch like. Whereof though I coulde fette downe manie: yet becaufe I want bothe manie and the beft kindes of them, I will ouerpaffe: onelie pointing you to one or two which may fuffice for example.

Looke vppon the rufull fong of *Colin* fung by *Cuddie* in the *Sheepheardes Calender*, where you fhall fee a finguler rare deuife of a dittie framed vpon thefe fixe wordes *VVoe, founde, cryes, paЯ, fleep, augment*, which are moft prettilie turned and wounde vppe mutually together, expreffing wonderfully the dolefulneffe of the fong. A deuife not much vnlike vnto the fame, is vfed by fome, who taking the laft wordes of a certaine number of verfes, as it were by the rebound

E

of an *Echo*, fhall make them fall out in fome prettie fence.

Of this forte there are fome deuifed by *Iohn Graunge*, which becaufe they be not long I wyll rehearfe one.

> If feare oppreffe howe then may hope me fhielde?
> Denyall fayes, vayne hope hath pleafed well,
> But as fuch hope thou wouldeft not be thine,
> **So** would I not the like to rule my hart.
> **For** if **thou loueft it** bidds thee graunt forthwith
> Which is the ioy whereof I liue in hope.

Here if you take the laft worde of euerie verfe, and place them orderlie together, you fhall haue this fentence: *Shielde well thyne hart with hope*. But of thefe *Echoes* I knowe indeede verie daintie peeces of worke, among fome of the fineft Poets this day in London: who for the rareneffe of them keepe them priuelie to themfelues, and wil not let them come abroad.

A like inuention **to** the laft rehearfed, or rather a better, haue I feene often practifed in framing a whole dittie to the Letters **of** ones name, or to the wordes of fome two or three verfes which is very witty, as for example this is one of *W. Hunnis*, which for the fhortnes I rather chufde then fome yat are better.

> If thou defire to liue in (quiet) reft,
> Gyue eare and fee, but fay the beft.

Thefe two verfes are nowe as **it** were refolued into dyuers other, euery two wordes or fillables being the beginning of an other like verfe, in this fort.

If thou	delight in quietnes of life,
Defire	to fhunne from brawles, debate and ftrife :
To liue	in loue with G O D, with freend and foe,
In rest	fhalt fleepe when other cannot fo.
Gyue care	to **all**, yet doo not all beleeue,
And fee	the end and then thy fentence gyue :
But fay	For trueth of happy liues affignde
The best	hath he that quiet is in minde.

English Poetrie.

Thus are there infinite sortes of fine conueiances (as they may be termed) to be vsed, and are much frequented by versifyers, as well in composition of their verse, as the wittines of their matter: which all I will referre to the consideration of euerie pleasant headded Poet in their proper gifts: onelie I sett downe these fewe sortes of their formes of versifying, which may stand in steede to declare what manie others may be deuised in like sorte.

But nowe to proceede to the reformed kind of English verse which manie haue before this, attempted to put in practise, and to establish for an accustomed right among English Poets, you shall heare in like manner my simple iudgment concerning the same.

I am fully and certainlie perswaded, that if the true kind of versifying in immitation of Greekes and Latines, had beene practised in the English tongue, and put in vre from time to tyme by our Poets, who might haue continually beene mending and pollyshing the same, euery one according to their seuerall giftes: it would long ere this haue aspyred to as full perfection, as in anie other tongue whatsoeuer. For why may I not thinke so of our English, seeing that among the Romaines a long time, yea euen till the dayes of *Tully*, they esteemed not the Latine Poetrie almost worth any thing, in respecte of the Greeke, as appeareth in the Oration *pro Archia Poeta*: yet afterwardes it increased in credite more and more, and that in short space: so that in *Virgilles* time, wherein were they not comparable with the Greekes? So likewise, now it seemeth not currant for an English verse to runne vpon true quantity, and those feete which the Latines vse, becaue it is straunge, and the other barbarous custome, beeing within compasse of euery base witt, hath worne it out of credite or estimation. But if our wryters, beeing of learning and iudgment, would rather infringe thys curious custome, then omitte the occasion of inlarging the credite of their natiue speeche, and theyr owne prayses, by practising that commendable kind of wryting in true verse: then no doubt, as in other partes of learning, so in Poetry, shoulde not stoupe to the best of them all in all maner of ornament and comlinesse. But some obiect that our wordes are nothing resemblaunt in nature to theirs, and therefore not possible to bee framed with any good grace after their vse: but cannot we then as well as the Latines did, alter the cannon of the rule according to the quality of our worde, and where our wordes and theyrs wyll agree, there to iumpe with them, where they will not agree, there to establish a rule of our owne to be directed by? Likewise, for ye tenor of the verse might we not (as *Horace* dyd in the Latine) alter their proportions to what sortes we listed, and to what we sawe wold best become the nature of the thing handled, or the quallity of the words? Surely it is to be thought that if any one, of sound iudgment and learning, shoulde putt foorth some famous worke, contayning dyuers formes of true verses, fitting the measures, according to the matter: it would of it selfe be a sufficient authority without any prescription of rules, to the most part of Poets, for them to follow and by custome to ratify. For sure it is, that the rules and principles of Poetry, were not precisely followed and obserued of the first beginners and wryters of Poetry, but were selected and gathered seuerally out of theyr workes, for the direction and behoofe of their followers. And indeede, he that shall with heedefull iudgment make tryall of the English wordes, shall not finde them so grosse or vnapt, but that they wyll become any one of ye most accustomed sortes of Latine or Greeke verses meetely, and run thereon somewhat currantly.

I my selfe, with simple skyll I confesse, and farre vnable iudgment, haue ventured on a fewe, which notwithstanding the rudenes of them may serue to shewe what better might bee brought into our speeche, if those which are of meete abilitye woulde bestowe some trauell and endeuour thereuppon. But before I sette them downe, I wyll speake somewhat of such obseruations as

I could gather neceſſary to the knowledge of theſe kinde of verſes, leaſt I ſhould ſeeme to runne vpon them raſhly, without regarde either of example or authority.

The ſpeciall poyntes of a true verſe, are the due obſeruations of the feete, and place of the feete.

The foote of a verſe, is a meaſure of two fillables, or of three, diſtinguiſhed by time which is eyther long or ſhort. A foote of two fillables, is eyther ſimple or mixt, that is, of like time or of diuers. A ſimple foote of two fillables is likewiſe twofolde, eyther of two long fillables called *Spondæus*, as − − *goodneſſe*, or of two ſhort called *Pyrrichius* as ◡ ◡ *hyther*. A myxt foote of 2. fillables, is eyther of one ſhort and one long called *Iambus* as ◡ − *dying*: or of one long and one ſhort, called *Choreus* as − ◡ *gladly*. A foote of 3. fillables in like forte is either ſimple or myxt. The ſimple is eyther *Moloſſus*, that is of three long, as − − − *forgiuenes*: or *Trochæus*, that is of 3. ſhort, as ◡ ◡ ◡ *merylie*. The mixt is of 6. diuers ſortes, 1. *Dactylus*, of one long, and two ſhort, as − ◡ ◡ *happily*. 2. *Anapæſtus*, of two ſhorte, and one long, as ◡ ◡ − *t[r]auelers*. 3. *Bacchius*, of one ſhort, and two long, as ◡ − − *remembrers*. 4. *Palimbachius*, of two long and one ſhort, as − − ◡ *accorded*. 5. *Creticus* of a long, a ſhort, and a long, − ◡ − *daungerous*. 6. *Amphibrachus*, of a ſhort, a long, and a ſhort, as ◡ − ◡ *reioyced*.

Many more deuiſions of feete are vſed by ſome, but theſe doo more artificially comprehende all quantities neceſſary to the ſkanning of any verſe, according to *Tallæus* in hys Rethorique. The place of the feete is the diſpoſing of them in theyr propper roomes, whereby may be diſcerned the difference of eche verſe which is the right numbring of the ſame. Now as for the quantity of our wordes, therein lyeth great difficultye, and the cheefeſt matter in this faculty. For in truth there being ſuch diuerſity betwixt our words and the Latine, it cannot ſtande indeede with great reaſon that they ſhoulde frame, wee beeing onelie directed by ſuch rules as ſerue for onely Latine words, yet notwithſtanding one may well perceiue by theſe fewe, that theſe kinde of verſes would well become the ſpeeche, if ſo bee there were ſuch Rules preſcribed, as woulde admitt the placing of your apteſt and fulleſt wordes together. For indeede excepting a fewe, of our *Monaſyllables*, which naturally ſhoulde moſt of them be long, we haue almoſt none, that wyll ſtande fitlie in a ſhort foote: and therfore if ſome exception were made againſt the preciſe obſeruation of *Poſition*, and certaine other of the rules, then might we haue as great plenty and choyſe of good woordes to furniſh and ſette foorth a verſe, as in any other tongue.

Likewiſe if there were ſome derection in ſuch wordes, as fall not within the compaſſe of Greeke or Latine rules, it were a great helpe, and therefore I had great miſſe in theſe few which I made. Such as is the laſt ſillable in theſe wordes, *able, noble,* or *poſſible* and ſuch like: againe for the nature and force of our *W.* of our *th*, of our *oo*, and *ee*, of our wordes which admytte an *e* in the ende after one or two Conſonantes, and many other. I for my part, though (I muſt needes confeſſe) many faultes eſcaped me in theſe fewe, yet tooke I as good heede as I coulde, and in trueth did rather alwaies omitt the beſt wordes and ſuch as would naturally become the ſpeech beſt, then I wolde committe any thing, which ſhoulde notoriouſly impugne the Latine rules, which herein I had onely for my direction. Indeede moſt of our *Monaſyllables* I am forced to make ſhort, to ſupply the want of many ſhort wordes requiſite in theſe verſes. The Participle *A*, being but the Engliſh article adioyned to Nownes, I always make ſhort, both alone and in compoſition, and likewiſe the wordes of one ſillable ending in *E*, as *the*, when it is an article, *he, ſhe, ye,* etc. *we* I thinke ſhould needes be alwayes long becauſe we pronounce continually *VVe. I,* beeing alone ſtanding for the Pronowne *Ego*, in my iudgment might well be vſed common: but becauſe I neuer ſawe it vſed but ſhort I ſo obſerued it. Words ending in *y*

Englifh Poetrie.

I make fhort without doubt, fauing that I haue marked in others one difference which they vfe in the fame, that is to make it fhort in the ende of an Aduerb, as *gladly*, and long in the ende – of an Adiectiue as *goodly*: but the reafon is as I take it, becaufe the Adiectiue is or fhould be moft commonly written thus *goodlie*. *O*, beeing an **Aduerbe** is naturally long: in the ende of wordes both ***Mona****fyllables* and other I thinke it may be vfed **common.** The firft of *Pollifyllables* I directed according to the nature of the worde, as I thought moft auniwerable to Latine examples, fauing that fomewhere I am conftrayned to ftraine curtefy with the prepofition of a worde compounded or fuch like, which breaketh no great fquare: as in *defence* or *depart*, etc. The myddle fillables which are not very many, come for the moft part vnder the precinct of *Pofition*, whereof fome of them will not poffibly abide the touch, and therfore muft needes be a little wrefted: fuch are commonly ye Aduerbs of three fillables, as *mournfully*, *fpyghtfully* and fuch like words, deriued of this Adiectiue, *full*: and therfore if there be great occafion to vfe them, they muft be reformed by detracting onely (*l*) and then they ftand meetely currant, as *mournfuly*. The laft fillables I wholly directed fo neere as I could to the touch of common rules.

The moft famous verfe of all the reft, is called *Hexametrum Epicum*, which confifteth of fixe feete, wherof the firft foure are indifferently either *Spondæi* or *Dactyli*, the fift is euermore a *dactyl*, aud the fixt a *Spondæ*, as thus.

— ͜ ͜ — ͜ ͜ — — — — — ͜ ͜ — —

Tyterus happily thou liest tumbling vnder a beetchtree.

Thys kinde of verfe I haue onely feene to be practifed in our Englifh fpeeche: and indeede wyll ftand fomewhat more orderlye therein then any of the other kindes, vntill we haue fome tolleration of wordes made by fpeciall rule. The firft that attempted to practife thys verfe in Englifh, fhould feeme to be the Earle of **Surry,** who tranflated fome part of *Virgill* into verfe indeede, but without regard of true quantity of fillables. There is one famous *Distichon*, which is common in the mouthes of all men, that was made by one Master *VVatson*, fellowe of **S.** *Iohns* Colledge in Cambrydge about 40. yeeres past, which for the fweetnes and gallantnes therof in all refpects doth mat[c]h and furpaffe the Latine coppy of *Horace*, which he made out of *Homers* wordes, *qui mores hominum etc.*

— ‿ ‿ — — — ‿ ‿ — — — — ‿ ‿ — —
All trauellers **doo** *gladlie report great praife to* **Uliſſes**

— ‿ ‿ — ‿ ‿ — — — — — ‿ ‿ — —
For that he knewe manie mens maners, and favv many citties.

Which two verfes **if they be** examined throughout all the rules and obferuations **of** the beft verfifying, fhall bee founde to **attaine** the very perfection of them all. There be two **other** not much inferiour **to** thefe, which I found in ye **Gloffe** of *E. K.* vppon the **fift** *Æglogue* of the newe **Poet:** which Tully tranflated out of Greeke into Latine, *Hæc habui quæ edi etc.*

All that I eate **did I ioy and all** *that I greedilie gorged.*

— — — ‿ ‿ — — — — — ‿ ‿ — —
As for *thofe manie goodlie matters left* **I** *for others.*

Which though they **wyll not** abide **the** touch **of** *Synalæpha* in one or two places, yet perhappes fome Englifh rule which might wyth good reafon be eftablifhed, would make them currant enough, and auoyde **that** inconuenience which is very obuious in our wordes. The great company of famous verfes of thys fort, which Mafter *Haruey* made, **is not** vnknowne **to** any and are to be viewed at all times. I for my part, fo farre as thofe examples would leade me, and mine owne fmall fkyll affoorde **me, haue** blundered vppon thefe fewe, whereinto I **haue** tranflated the two firft Æglogues of **Virgill:** becaufe I thought no matter of mine owne **inuention,** nor any other of antiquitye more fitte for tryal of thys thyng, before there were fome more fpeciall direction, which might leade to a leffe trou ··· ·me manner of wryting.

The Argument of the firſt
Æglogue.

Vnder the perſonne of *Tityrus Vyrgill* beeing figured himſelfe, declareth to *Melibeus* an nother Neateheard, the great
benefittes he receyued at *Auguſtus* hand, who in the ſpoyle
of *Mantua* gaue him hys goods and ſubſtaunce againe.

Melibæus.   Tityrus.

TItyrus, *happilie thou lyſte tumbling vnder* **a beech tree**,
   All in a fine oate pipe theſe ſweete **ſongs** *luſtilie chaunting:*
VVe, *poore ſoules goe to wracke, and from theſe coaſtes beremooued,*
And *fro our paſtures ſvveete:* **thou** *Tityr, at eaſe in a ſhade plott*
Makſt *thicke groues to* **reſound vvith** *ſonges of braue* Amarillis.

Tityrus.

O Melibæus, *he vvas no man but a God vvho* **releeude me:**
Euer *he ſhalbe my God: from this ſame Sheepcot his alters*
Neuer, *a tender Lambe ſhall vvant, vvith blood to bedevv them.*
This *good gift did he giue, to my ſteeres thus freelie to vvander,*
And *to my ſelfe (thou ſeeſt) on pipe to reſound vvhat J liſted.*

Melibaeus.

Grutch thee sure I doo not, but this thing makes me to wonder,
Whence comes all this adoo: with grieeuous paine not a little
Can I remooue my Goates: here, Tityre skant get I forward
Poore olde crone, two twyns at a clappe ith boysterous hasiles
Left she *behind, best* **hope i'** *my flock laid hard* **on a bare** *stone.*
Had not *a luckleffe* **lotte** *possest our mindes, I remember*
Warnings oft fro the blast burnt oake **we saw to be sent vs.**
Oft did a *left hand* **crow** *foretell* **these** *thinges in* **her hull tree,**
But *this God let vs heare what he was, good Tityre* **tell me.**

Tityrus.

That *same Cittie so braue which Rome was* **wont to be** *called,*
Foole did I thinke, to be like this of ours, where we to the pastures
Wonted were to remooue from dammes our young prettie Cattell.
Thus did J thinke young whelpes, and Kids to be like to the mothers,
Thus did I wont compare manie great thinges with many little.
But this aboue **all townes as loftily** *mounteth her high head,*
As by the lowe base shrubbes **tall** *Cypresse shooteth aboue them.*

Melibaeus.

And what did thee mooue that needes thou must goe to see Rome?

Tityrus.

Freedome: *which though late, yet once lookt backe to my pore state,*
After time when haires from my beard did ginne to be whitish:
Yet lookt back at last and found me out after a long time.
When Amarill *was once obtainde,* Galatea *departed:*
For (for I will confesse) whilst as Galatea *did hold mee,*
Hope did I not for freedome, and **care had I** *none to my cattell.*
Though **manie** *faire young beastes* **our** *folde for the aulters aforded*

English Poetrie.

And **manie cheefes** good fro my preſſe vvere ſent to the Cittie:
Seldome times did I bring anie store of pence fro the markett.

Melibaeus.

O Amarill, vvherefore, to thy Gods (very much did I meruaile)
Heauilie thou didſt praie: ripe fruites vngathered all still:
Tityrus is not at home: theſe Pyne trees Tityre miſt **thee**.
Fountaines longd for thee: theſe hedgrovves vvisht **thy** return
   home

Tityrus.

VVhat **vvas** then to be doone? from bondage **could not** I vvind out:
Neither I could haue found ſuch gentle **Gods any vvhere** els.
There did **I** ſee (Melibœe) that youth **vvhoſe hestes I by** courſe
   still.
Fortnights whole to obſerue on the Alters sure will I not faile.
Thus did he gentlie graunt to my ſute when first I demaunded.
Keepe your heardes poore ſlaues as erst, let bulles to the makes
   still.

Melibaeus.

Happy olde man, then thou ſhalt haue thy farme to remaine still,
Large and large to thy ſelfe, others nought but stonie grauell:
And foule ſlymie rush wherewith their lees be beſprinkled.
Here no vnwoonted foode ſhall grieue young theaues who **be**
   laded,
Nor the infections foule of neighbours **flocke** ſhall annoie them.
Happie olde man. **In** ſhaddowy bankes and coole prettie places,
Heere by the quainted floodes **and** ſprings most holie remaining.
Here, theſe quickſets freſh which lands ſeuer out fro thy
   neighbors
And greene willow rowes which Hiblœ bees doo reioice in,
Oft fine whistring noiſe, ſhall bring ſweete ſleepe to thy fences.
Vnder a Rock ſide here will proyner chaunt merrie ditties.
Neither on highe Elme trees, thy beloude Doues loftilie fitting,
Nor prettie Turtles trim, vvill ceaſe **to** crooke with a good cheere.

Tityrus.

First, therefore swift **buckes shall flie for foode to the** *skies ward,*
And from fish with drawn broade seas themselues shal **auoid**
  hence:
First, (both borders broke) Araris shal run to the Parthanes,
And likewise Tygris shall againe runne backe to the Germanes:
Ere his countnaunce sweete shall slippe once out from my **hart roote.**

Melibaeus.

VVe poore soules, must *some to the land cald Affrica* **packe hence.**
Some to the farre Scythia, and some must **to the** *swift flood Oaxis.*
Some to Britannia coastes quite parted farre fro the whole world.
Oh these pastures **pure** *shall I nere more chance to behold yee?*
And our cottage poore with warme **turues couerd** *about trim.*
Oh these trim tilde landes, shall a rechlesse souldier haue them?
And shall **a** *Barbarian haue this croppe? see what a* **mischiefe**
Discord vile hath araisde? for whom was our labour **all** *tooke?*
Novv Melibœe ingraft pearie stocks, sette vines **in an** *order.*
Now *goe (***my** *braue flocke* **once that were***) O now goe* **my**
  kidlings.
Neuer againe *shall I now in a greene bowre sweetelie reposed*
See ye in queachie briers farre a loose clambring on a high hill.
Now shall I sing no Iygges, nor whilst I doo fall to my iunkets.
Shall ye my Goates, cropping sweete flowres **and** *leaues sit*
  about me.

Tityrus.

Yet thou maist tarrie heere, and keepe me companie this night,
All on a leauie couch: good Aples ripe I doo not lacke,
Chestnutts sweete good store, and plentie of curddes will I set thee.
Marke i' the Towne how chimnie tops doo beginne to be smoaking,
And *fro* **the** *Mountaines high how shaddowes grow to be larger.*

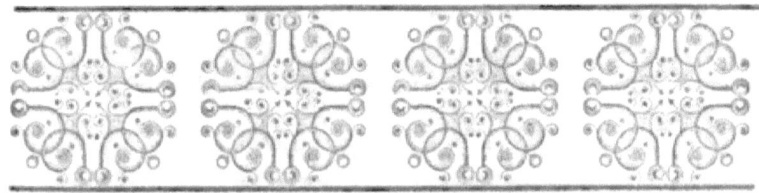

The feconde Æglogue called *Alexis*.

The Argument.

Virgill in the perfonne of *Corydon* as fome thinke, complayneth that he is not fo gratious with Auguftus as he would bee: or els it is to be referred to a youth *Alexander*, which was giuen him of *Afinius Pollio*, whom he blameth for the vnftedfaftnes of his witt and wandering appetite, in refufing the freendly counfayle which he vfed to giue him.

THat Sheepheard Corydon did burne in loue with Alexis,
 All his maftersdeare: and nought had hewherebytohope
Onely in beechen groues, and dolefome fhaddowy places. [for.
Dailie reforted he: there thefe rude difordered outcryes,
Hylles and defert woodes throughout thus mournfully tuned.
O hard harted Alex, haft thou no regard to my fweete fong?
Pyttieft me not a whitt: yea makft me now that I fhall dye.
Yet doo the beaftes find out fine fhades and trim pretty
 coole plottes,
And fro the fun beames fafe lie lyzardes vnder a bufhtufte:
And for workmen toughe with boyling heate fo beparched,
Garlick fauery fweete and coole hearbes plenty be dreffed.
But, by the fcorcht banke fydes i' thy foote fteppes ftil I goe
 plodding.

Hedgerowes hott doo resound with Grashops mournfully squeak-
O had I not ben better abyd Amarillis her anger? [ing,
And her proude disdaine? yea better abyde my Menalcas?
What though brown did he seeme? yea what though thou be
   so gallant
O thou fine **chery** cheekt child **truſt nót** t' much to thy beauty.
Black violetts are tooke when dayſes white be refuſed.
Me thou doſt deſpiſe vnknowne to thy ſelfe yet Alexis:
What be my riches greate in neate, in milke what aboundance.
In Sicill hylles be **my** Lambes of which there wander a thouſand.
All times, colde and hote yet freſh milke neuer I wanted.
Such be my Muſicke notes, as (when his flockes he recalling)
Amphion of Dirce did vſe on ſhore Aracynthus.
Much miſhapt I am not, for late in a bancke I behelde me,
VVhen ſtill ſeas were calme, to thy Daphnis neede not I giue
   place
No, though thou be the iudge, if pictures haue any credite.
O were thou content to remaine with me by the downes heere,
In theſe lodgings ſmall, and helpe me proppes to put vnder,
And trym kydling flocke with me to driue to the greene fieldes:
Pan in ſinging ſweete with me ſhouldſt brauely reſemble:
Pan, was firſt the inuenter, pypes to adioyne in an order:
Pan, poore flockes and Sheepheardes to moſt duly regardeth.
Thoſe fine lips thou needſt not feare to bruſe with a ſweete pype:
VVhat dyd Amynt forſake i'this excerciſe to be cunning?
One pype with ſeauene ſundry ſtops matcht ſweetly together.
Haue I my ſelfe, Damætas which ats death he bequeathd me,
And ſayd, heere, thou art now the ſecond which euer hath ought
So ſayd Damætas: but Amyntas ſpightfully ſcornde it. [it.
Alſo, two pretty ſmall wyld kyddes, moſt goodlie beſpotted
Haue I, that heere i' the dales doo runne skant ſafe I doo
   feare me.
Twyce in a day two teates they ſuck: for thee will I keepe them:
Wondrous faine to haue had them both was Theſtylis of late.
And ſo ſhe ſhall: for I ſee thou ſcornſt whatſo-euer I giue thee.
Come hyther O thou ſweete face boy: ſee ſee, to thy ſelfe heere
How fayre Nymphes in baskets full doo bring manie Lillies:
White violets ſweete Nais plucks and bloomes fro the Poppies,
Narcyſs, and dyll flowres moſt ſweete that fauoureth alſo.

Cafia, **broade** mary Goldes, with pancyes, and Hyacinthus.
And **I** my felfe rype peaches foft as filke will I gather.
And **fuch** Chefnutts as Amarill **was** wont **to** reioyce at.
Ploms wyll **I** bring likewife: that fruite fhall **be** honored alfo.
And ye O Lawrell twygges **that I** croppe, **and** myrte thy felfe next.
For ye be wont, (bound both in **a** bunch) moft **fweetely to** fauour.
Thou art but **a Clowne Corydon: thefe** gifts efteemes not Alexis:
Nor by thy gifts **to obtaine art meete** to incounter Iolas.
VVretch (ahlas) whats **this that I** wifh? fouth blafts **to** the yong flowers
Or cleere cryftall ftreames with loathfome fwyne **to be troubled.**
Ah **mad boy** from whom dooft runne? why Gods **ithe** woods dwelt:
And **Paris** erft of Troy: Pallas **moft gladly reioyfeth,**
In **thefe** bowres: and in trym **groues we all** chiefely delight vs.
Grym Lyoneffe doth courfe curft woolues, **fo** wolues doo the kydlinges.
And thefe wanton Kyddes likewife thefe **faire Cytifus** flowers.
Thee Corydon (O Alex) fome pleafure euery wight pulles.
See thefe yoked fteeres **fro** the plough nowe feeme to be lett loofe.
And thefe fhadowes large **doo declare** thys fun **to depart** hence
Styll I doo burne in loue. What meane in loue to be lookt **for?**
Ah **Corydon** Corydon, what raging fury dooth haunt thee,
Halfe **cropt** downe **be** thy vynes and broade braunckt elmes ouerhang them.
Rather **about fome** needefull worke **now** bufy thy felfe well,
Either on Ofyers tuffe or bulrufh weaue pretty basketts.
And if Alexis fcorne thee ftill, mayft hope for another.

FINIS.

I durst not enterpryse to goe any further with this rude translation: beeing for the respects aforesayd a troublesome and vnpleasant peece of labour: And therefore these shall suffice till further occasion shall serue to imploy some profitable paynes in this behalfe.

The next verse in dignity to the *Hexameters*, is ye *Carmen Elegiacum* which consisteth of foure feete and two od sillables: viz: the two first feete, eyther *Dactyli* or *Spondæi* indifferent, the one long sillable: next two *Dactyli* and an other long sillable – – – ◡ ◡ – – ◡ ◡ – ◡ ◡ – some doo measure it in this sorte (and more truely yet not so readily to all) accounting first two indifferently either *Dactyli* or *Spondæi*, then one *Spondæi*, and two *Anapæsti*. But it commeth all to one reckoning. Thys verse is alwayes vnseperably adioyned vnto the Hexameter, and serueth especially to the handling of loue and dalliances, whereof it taketh the name. It will not frame altogether so currantlye in our English as the other, because the shortnesse of the seconde *Penthimimer* will hardly be framed to fall together in good sence, after the Latine rules. I haue not seene very many of them made by any, and therefore one or two for example sake shall be sufficient.

This *Distichon* out of *Ouid*.

> *Ingenium quondam fuerat pretiosius auro,*
> *At nunc barbaries grandis habere nihil.*

May thus be translated.

Learning once was thought to be better then any gold was,
Now he that hath not wealth is but a barbarian.

And thys

> *Omnia sunt hominum tenui pendentia filo:*
> *Et subito casu quæ valuere ruunt.*

Tis but a slender thread, which all mens states do depend on:
And most goodly thinges quickly doo fall to decay.

Englifh Poetrie.

As for the verfes *Phalocium* and *Iambicum*, I haue not as yet made any tryall in them: but the *Sapphic* I affure you, in my iudgment wyl doo very pretty, if ye wants which I fpeake were once fupplied. For tryall of which I haue turned the new Poets fweete fong of *Eliza* into fuch homely *Sapphick* as I coulde.

Thys verfe confifteth of thefe fiue feete, one *Chore*, one *fpondæ*, one *dactyl*, and two *Choreis*, with this addition, that after euery third verfe be fette one *Adonium* verfe, which confifteth of a *dactyl* and a *fpondæ*. It is more troublefome and tedious to frame in our fpeeche by reafon they runne without difference, euery verfe being a like in quantity throughout, yet in my iudgement ftandeth meetely well in the fame. I pray looke the Coppy which I haue tranflated in the fourth *Æglogue* of the *Sheepheardes Calender*: ye fong of *Colins* making which *Hobbinoll* fingeth in prayfe of the Queenes maiefty, vnder the name of *Eliza*.

YE dainty Nymphes that in this bleffed brooke,
    doo bathe your breft:
Forfake your watry bowres and hether looke,
    at my requeft:
And onely you Virgins that on *Parnafs* dwell.
Whence floweth *Helicon* the learned well,
    helpe me to blafe
    her worthy praife
That in her fex doth all excell.

Of fayre *Eliza* be your filuer fong
    that bleffed wight:
The flowre of Virgins, may fhe flourifh long,
    in princely plight.
For fhe is *Syrinx* daughter without fpott,
Which *Pan* the Sheepheards God on her begot:
    fo fprang her grace,
    of heauenly race,
No mortall blemifh may her blott.

See where fhe fittes, etc.

A Discourse of

The *Saphick* verse.

```
— ⏑ — — — ⏑ ⏑ — ⏑ — —
— ⏑ — — — ⏑ ⏑ — ⏑ — —
— ⏑ — — — ⏑ ⏑ — ⏑ — —
            — ⏑ ⏑ — —
```

O ye Nymphes most fine who resort to this brooke,
 For to bathe there your pretty breasts at all times :
Leaue the watrish bowres, hyther and to me come
  at my request nowe.

And ye Virgins trymme who resort to *Parnafs*,
Whence the learned well *Helicon* beginneth :
Helpe to blase her worthy deserts, that all els
  mounteth aboue farre.

Nowe the siluer songes of *Eliza* sing yee,
Princely wight whose peere not among the virgins
Can be found : that long she may remaine among vs.
  now let vs all pray.

For *Syrinx* daughter she is, of her begotten
Of the great God *Pan*, thus of heauen aryseth,
All her exlent race : any mortall harde happe
  cannot aproche her.

See, she sittes most seemely in a grassy greene plott,
Clothed in weedes meete for a princely mayden,
Boste with Ermines white, in a goodly scarlett
  brauely beseeming.

Decked is that crowne that vpon her head standes
With the red Rose and many Daffadillies,
Bayes, the Primrose and violetts, be sette by : how
  ioyfull a sight ist.

Say, behold did ye euer her Angelike face,
Like to *Phœbe* fayre ? or her heauenly hauour
And the princelike grace that in her remaineth ?
  haue yee the like seene ?

Medled ist red rose with a white together
Which in either cheeke do depeinct a trymme cheere,
Her maiestie and eye to behold so comely, her
  like who remembreth ?

English Poetrie.

Phœbus once peept foorth with a goodly guilt hewe,
For **to gaze**: but when he fawe the bright beames
Spread abroade fro' her face with a glorious grace,
                        it did **amaze** him.

When another funne he behelde belowe heere,
Blufht he red for fhame, nor againe he durft looke:
Would he durft bright beames of his owne with hers match,
                        for to be vanquifht.

Shew thy felfe **now** *Cynthia* with thy cleere rayes,
And behold **her**: neuer abafht be thou fo: [beauty, how
When fhe fpreades thofe beames of her heauenly
                      thou **art in a** dump dafht?

But **I will take** heede that I match not **her grace**,
With the *Laton* feede, *Niobe* that once did,
Nowe fhe doth therefore in a ftone **repent: to all**
                        other a warning.

Pan he may well boafte that he **did begit her**
Such a noble wight, **to** *Syrinx* is it ioy,
That fhe found fuch **lott** with a bellibone **trym**
                      for to be loaden.

When my younglinges firft to the dammes doo bleat out,
Shall a milke white Lambe to my Lady be offred: [grome.
For **my Godd**effe fhee is yea I my felfe her Heard-
                    though **but a rude** Clowne.

Vnto that **place** *Caliope* dooth high **her,**
Where my Goddeffe fhines: **to** the fame **the** Mufer
After her with fweete Violines about them
                      cheerefully tracing

Is not it Bay braunche that **aloft in** handes they haue,
Eune to giue them fure to **my Lady** *Eliza*:
O fo fweete **they** play—and to the fame doo fing too
                      heauuly to heare ift.

See, the Graces trym to the ftroake doo foote it,
Deftly dauncing, and meriment doo make them,
Sing to the inftruments to reioyce the more, but
                    wants not a fourth grace?

Then the daunce wyll be eune, to my Lady therefore
Shalbe geune that place, for a grace she shall be
For to fill that place that among them in heaune, she
                                      may be receiued.
Thys beuy of bright Nymphes, whether ist goe they now?
Raunged all thus fine in a rowe together?
They be Ladies all i' the Lake behight soe?
                                  they thether all goe.
One that is there chiefe that among the rest goes,
Called is *Chores* of Olyues she beares a
Goodly Crownett, meete for a Prince that in peace
                                        euer abideth.
All ye Sheepheardes maides that about the greene dwell,
Speede ye there to her grace, but among ye take heede
All be Virgins pure that aproche to deck her,
                                    duetie requireth.
When ye shall present ye before her in place,
See ye not your selues doo demeane too rudely:
Bynd the fillets: and to be fine the waste gyrt
                                  fast with a tawdryne
Bring the Pinckes therewith many Gelliflowres sweete,
And the Cullambynes: let vs haue the Wynesops,
With the Cornation that among the loue laddes
                                wontes to be worne much.
Daffadowndillies all a long the ground strowe,
And the Cowslyppe with a prety paunce let heere lye.
Kyngcuppe and Lillies so beloude of all men
                                  And the deluce flowre.

    One verse there remaineth vntranslated as yet, with some other of this sorte, which I meant to haue finished, but by reason of some let which I had, I am constrained to defer to some other time, when I hope to gratify the Readers with more and better verses of this sort: for in trueth I am perswaded a little paine taking might furnish our speeche with as much pleasaunt delight in this kinde of verse, as any other whatsoeuer.

Englifh Poetrie.

Heere followe the Cannons or generall cautions of Poetry, prefcribed by Horace, firft gathered by *Georgius Fabricius Cremnicenfis*: which I thought good to annex to thys Treatife, as very neceffary obferuations to be marked of all Poets.

In his Epiftle ad Pifones
de arte Poetica.

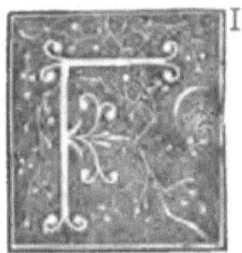Irft let the inuention be meete for the matter, not differing, or ftraunge, or monftrous. For a womans head, a horfe necke, the bodie of a dyuers coloured Byrd, and many members of fundry creatures compact together, whofe legges ending like a Fyfhes tayle: this in a picture is a wonderful deformitie : but if there be fuch diuerfitye in the frame of a fpeeche, what can be more vncomely or ilfauoured?

2. The ornaments or colours muft not bee too many, nor rafhly aduentured on, neither muft they be vfed euery where and thruft into euery place.

3. The proprietie of fpeeche muft bee duely obferued that wayghty and great matters be not fpoken flenderly, or matters of length too briefly: for it belongeth much both to the comlineffe and nature of a matter: that

in big matters there be lykewife vfed boyfterous wordes.

4. In Poeticall defcriptions, the fpeeche muft not exceede all credite, nor any thing fainedlie brought in, againft all courfe of nature.

5. **The** difpofing of the worke **muft be fuch,** that **there be** no offence committed, as it were **by too ex-quifite** dilligence: for many thinges may be oft **committed, and fome** thing by **too** curious **handling be made** offenciue. Neyther is **it in** one part **to be well** furnifhed, **and** in another to be neglected. Which is **prooued** by example of a **Caruer,** who expreffed **very artificially** the heade **and vpper** part of a body, **but the reft hee** could not make an ende of. Againe, it is **prooued** thus, **that a body fhould not be** in other partes beautifull, and yet **bee deformed in the** crooked **nofe:** for all **the** members **in a well fhapen bodie muft be** aunfwerable, found, and well **proportioned.**

6. He that **taketh in hande to write any thing muft** firft **take heede that he be fufficient for the fame: for** often vnwary fooles **through their rafhnes are ouertooke** with great want **of ability**

7. The ornament **of a worke** confifteth in wordes, and in the manner **of the wordes,** are either fimple **or** mixt, newe or olde, propper **or** tranflated. In them all good iudgment muft be vfed **and ready wytt.** The chiefeft grace **is** in the moft frequented wordes, for the fame reafon holdeth in wordes, **as** doth in coynes, that the moft vfed **and tried are beft efteemed.**

8. The kinde of verfe is to be confidered **and** aptly **applied** to the **argument, in** what meafure **is** moft meete **for euery** fort. The moft vfuall kindes **are** foure, the *Heroic, Elegiac, Iambick,* and *Lyric.*

9. One muft vfe **one** kynde **of** fpeeche alike in **all** wrytings. Sometime the *Lyric* ryfeth aloft, **fometime** the comicall. **To the** Tragicall wryters belong properly the bygge and boyfterous **wordes.** Examples muft be interplaced according fitly **to the** time and place.

10. Regarde is to **be** had **of** affections: **one** thing

becommeth pleafant perfons, an other fadde, an other wrathfull, an other gentle, which muft all be heedefully refpected, Three thinges therefore are requifite in verfes, beauty, fweetnes, and the affection. *Theophraftus* fayth that this beauty or delectableneffe is a deceyt, and Ariftotle calleth it τυραννία ολιγοκρονίον, a momentany tyrany. Sweetneffe retayneth a Reader, affection moueth him.

11. Euery perfon muft be fitted accordingly, and the fpeeche well ordered: wherein are to be confidered the dignity, age, fex, fortune, condition, place, Country, etc. of eche perfon.

12. The perfonnes are eyther to be fayned by the Poets them felues, or borrowed of others, if he borrow them, then muft hee obferue το ὅμοιον, that is, that he folow that Author exactly whom he purpofeth to immitate, and whereout he bringeth his examples. But if he fayne newe perfonnes, then muft he keepe his το ὁμαλόν, that is equallie: fo bringing them in eche place, that it be alwayes agreeable, and the laft like vnto the firft, and not make one perfon nowe a bolde boafter, and the fame ftraightwaies a wife warie man, for that is paffing abfurd. Againe, euery one muft obferue το ἁρμοστον, which is interpreted *conuenientiam*, fitneffe: as it is meete and agreeable euery where, a man to be ftoute, a woman fearefull, a feruant crafty, a young man gentle.

13. Matters which are common may be handled by a Poet as they may be thought propper to himfelfe alone. All matters of themfelues are open to be intreated of by any man: but if a thing be handled of fome one in fuch fort, as he thereby obtaine great prayfe, he maketh it his owne or propper to himfelfe, as many did write of the Troiane war, but yet *Homer* made matter which was common to all, propper to himfelfe.

14. Where many thinges are to be taken out of auncienter tongues, as the Latines tooke much out of the Greekes, the wordes are not fo precifelie to be followed, but that they bee altered according to the iudg-

ment and will of the Immitator, **which** precept is borrowed of Tully, *Non verbum* ***verbo necesse*** *est reddere.*

15. The beginning muſt not be fooliſhly handled, that is, ſtraungly **or too** long.

16. The propoſition or **narration let it not be** far fetched or vnlikely, and in the ſame forget **not the** differences of ages and perſons.

17. In a Comedie it is needfull to **exhibite all the actions** openlie, as ſuch as are cruell, vnhoneſt, **or ougly, but ſuch thinges may** better bee declared by ſome meete and handſome wordes, after what ſorte they are **ſuppoſed to bee** doone.

18. If a Commedye haue **more** Actes then fiue, it **is tedious, if fewer**, it is not ſufficient.

It fytteth not to bring **in the** perſonnes of Gods, but in verie great matters. ***Cicero*** ſayth, when the Tra**gedy** wryters cannot bring theyr **matters** to good paſſe, **they** runne to God. Let not **more** perſonnes ſpeake together then foure for auoyding confuſion.

The *Chori* **muſt** be well garniſhed and ſette **foorth: wherein eyther menne are** admoniſhed, or reprehended, **or counſayled vnto vertue. Such matter** muſt bee choſen for the *Chorus*, **as may bee meete and** agreeable to that which is in hand. As for inſtruments and ſinging, **they are** Reliques of olde ſimplicitye. **For the Muſicke** commonlye vſed at Theaters and **the licencioufneſſe** of theyr ſonges, which together wyth **theyr wealth increaſed** among the Romaines, **is hurtfull to** diſcipline and good manners.

19. In a *Satyr* the clowniſh company and rurall Gods, **are** brought **in** to temperate the Heauineſſe of Trage**dies**, wyth **ſome** myrth **and paſtyme. In** ieſting it muſt be obſerued **that it bee not lacyuious or** Rybaldlike, or ſlaunderous, **which precept holdeth** generallie in all ſortes of wrytynges.

In a *Satyr* greate heede is to be taken, of the place, of the day, and of the perſonnes: as of *Bacchus, Silenus,* or the *Satyres.* Againe of the vnmeetneſſe or inconuenience of the matter, and of the wordes that they be fitted according to the persons: of *Decorum*, that he which represented some noble personage in the Tragedie, bee not some busy foole in the *Satyr*: finallie of the hearers, least they bee offended by myxing filthy matters with iestes, wanton toyes wyth vnhonest, or noysome with merry thinges.

20. The feete are to be applied propper to euery kinde of verse, and therin a Poet must not vse too much licence or boldnes. The auncient writers in *Iambick* verses vsed at first pure *Iambicks*: Afterwards *Spondæus* was admitted into *Locos impares*, but at last such was the licentious custome, that they woulde both *Spondæus* where they listed, and other feete without regarde.

21. In complying of verses great care and circumspection must be vsed.

Those verses which be made Extempore, are of no great estimation: those which are vnartificiall, are vtterly repelled as too foolish. Though many doo lightlie regard our verses, yet ought the Carelesnesse of the hearers to bee no cause in vs of errour and negligence. Who desireth to make any thing worthy to be heard of learned eares, let hym reade Greeke Authors heedefullie and continually.

22. Artes haue their increasinges euen as other things, beeing naturall, so haue Tragedies which were first rudely inuented by *Thespis*, at last were much adorned by *Æschylus*: at the first they were practised in Villages of the Countrey, afterwardes brought to stages in great Citties.

23. Some Artes doo increase, some doo decay by a certayne naturall course. The olde manner of Commedies decayde, by reason of slaundering which therein they vsed against many, for which there was a penaltie appointed, least their bitternes should proceede too farre: In place of which among the Latines came the *Satyres*.

The auncient Authors of Comedies, were *Eupolis*, *Cratinus*, and *Aristophanes*, of the middle sorte *Plato*

Comicus, of the laſt kinde *Menander*, which continued and was accounted the moſt famous.

24. A Poet ſhould not content himſelfe onely with others inuentions, but himſelfe alſo by ye example of old wryters ſholde bring ſomething of his owne induſtry, which may bee laudable. So did they which writte among the Latines the Comedies called *Togatæ*, whoſe arguments were taken from ye Greekes, and the other which wrytt the *Pretextatæ*, whereof the arguments were Latine.

25. Heedefulneſſe and good compoſition maketh a perfecte verſe, and that which is not ſo may be reprehended. The faculty of a goode witte exceedeth Arte.

26. A Poet that he may be perfect, hath neede to haue knowledge of that part of Philoſophy which informeth ye life to good manners. The other which pertaineth to naturall thinges, is leſſe plauſible, hath fewer ornaments, and is not ſo profitable.

27. A Poet to the knowledge of Philoſophie ſhoulde alſo adde greater experience, that he may know the faſhions of men and diſpoſitions of people. Thys profit is gott by trauelling, that whatſoeuer he wryteth he may ſo expreſſe and order it, that hys narration may be formable.

28. The ende of Poetry is to wryte pleaſant thinges, and profitable. Pleaſant it is which delighteth by beeing not too long, or vneaſy to be kept in memory, and which is ſomewhat likelie, and not altogether forged. Profitable it is, which ſtyrreth vppe the mindes to learning and wiſedome.

29. Certaine eſcapes are to be pardoned in ſome Poets, ſpecially in great workes. A faulte may bee committed either in reſpect of hys propper Arte, or in ſome other Arte: that a Poet ſhoulde erre in precepts of hys owne arte, is a ſhamefull thing, to committe a faulte in another Arte is to be borne withal: as in *Virgil*, who fayneth that *Æneas* comming into *Affrica* ſlew with hys darte certaine Stagges, whereas

indeede *Affrica* hath in it none of thofe beaftes. Such errours doo happen eyther by vnheedefulnes, when one efcapeth them by negligence: or by the common fragility of man, becaufe none there is which can know all thinges. Therefore this laft kinde of errour is not to be ftucke vppon.

30. A good Poet fhould haue refpect to thys, how to retaine hys Reader or hearer. In a picture fome thing delighteth beeing fette farre of, fomething nearer, but a Poet fhould delight in all places as well in funne as fhaddowe.

31. In a Poet is no meane to be admitted, which if hee bee not he of all is the worft of all.

32. A Poeme if it runne not fweetely and fmoothly is odious: which is proued by a *fimile* of the two fenfes, hearing and tafting, as in fweete and pleafaunt meates. And the Poem muft bee of that forte, that for the fweeteneffe of it may bee acceptable and continue like it felfe vnto the ende, leaft it wearye or driue away a Reader.

33. He that would wryte any thing worthy the pofteritye, let him not enterprife any thing wherevnto his nature is not agreeable. *Mercury* is not made of wood (as they fay) neyther doth *Minerua* fauour all ftudies in euery one. In all Artes nature is the beft helpe, and learned men vfe commonly to fay that *A Poet is as well borne as made a Poet.*

34. Let no man efteeme himfelfe fo learned, but that he may fubmytte hys wrytinges to the iudgments of others, and correct and throughly amend the fame himfelfe.

35. The profitte of Poetry fprang thus, for that the auncient wyfe men fet downe the beft things that pertained to mans life, manners, or felicity, and examining and proouing the fame by long experience of time, when they are aged they publifhed them in wrytinges. The vfe of Poetry what it was at the firft, is manifeft by the examples of the mofte learned men: as of *Orpheus* who firft builded houfes: of *Amphion* who

made Citties, of *Tyrtæus* who first made warre: of *Homer*, who wryt most wysely.

36. In an artificiall **Poet three** thinges are requisite, nature, Arte, and dilligence.

37. **A** wryter **must** learne **of** the learned, **and he must not** sticke **to** confesse when **he** erreth: that the **worse he may** learne to auoyde, **and knowe howe to follow** the better.

The confession of an errour betoken a noble and a gentle **minde.** *Celsus* and *Quintillian* doo report of *Hippocrates*, **that** least he should **deceiue** his posterity, he confessed certayne errours, as **it well** became an **excellent minded** man, and one of great credite. For (as sayth *Celsus*) light witts becaufe they haue nothing, **wyll haue** nothing taken **from** them.

38. **In** making choife **of such** freendes **as** should tell **vs** the trueth, and correct our wrytinges, **heedefull iudgment** must bee vsed: least eyther we choose **vn- skylfull folke, or** flatterers, **or** dissemblers. The vnskil- full **know not how to** iudge, flatterers feare to offende, dissemblers in not praysing doo seeme to commende.

39. **Let no** man deceiue himselfe, or suffer himselfe **to be** deceiued, but take some graue learned man to be **iudge of his** dooing, **and let** him according to hys counsayle change and put out what hee thinketh good.

40. He which will not flatter and is of ability **to** iudge, let him endeuour **to nothing so much, as to the correction of that** which is wrytten, and **that let be doone with** earnest and exquisite iudgment. He which **dooth not thus,** but offendeth wilfully in breaking his **credite too rashly, may be counted for a** madde, furious, and franticke **foole.**

41. **The** faultes commonly in verses **are** seauen, as either they be destitute of Arte, of facility, or ornament: or els, they be superfluous, obscure, ambicious, or needelesse.

Out of the Epiſtles ad Mecænatem, Auguſtum, et Florum.

42. An immitation ſhould not be too feruile or ſuperſtitious, as though one durſt not varry one iotte from the example: neyther ſhould it be ſo fenceleſſe or vnſkilfull, as to immitate thinges which are abſurde, and not to be followed.

43. One ſhould not altogether treade in the ſteppes of others, but ſometime he may enter into ſuch wayes as haue not beene haunted or vſed of others. *Horace* borrowed ye *Iambick* verſe of *Archilocus*, expreſſing fully his numbers and elegant[l]y, but his vnſeemely wordes and pratling tauntes hee moſte wyſhlye ſhunned.

44. In our verſes we ſhould not gape after the phraſes of the ſimpler ſorte, but ſtriue to haue our writings allowable in the iudgments of learned menne.

45. The common peoples iudgments of Poets is ſeldome true, and therefore not to be ſought after. The vulgar ſort in *Rome* iudged *Pacuuious* to be very learned, *Accius* to bee a graue wryter, that *Affranius* followed *Menander*, *Plautus*, *Epicharmus*: that *Terence* excelled in Arte *Cæcilius* in grauity: but the learned ſorte were not of this opinion. There is extant in *Macrobius* (I knowe not whether *Angellius*) the like verdite concerning them which wryt *Epigrammes*. That *Catullus* and *Caluus* wrytt fewe thinges that were good, *Næuius* obſcure, *Hortenſius* vncomely, *Cynna* vnpleaſant, and *Memmius* rough.

46. The olde wryters are ſo farre to be commended, as nothing be taken from the newe: neyther may we thinke but that the way lyeth open ſtyll to others to

attaine to as great matters. Full well fayd *Sidonius* to *Eucherius*, I reuerence the olde wryters, yet not fo as though I leffe efteemed the vertues and defertes of the wryters in this age.

47. **Newnes** is **gratefull if it be** learned: **for** certaine it is, **Artes are** not **bothe** begunne and perfected at **once, but are** increafed **by** time and ftudie, which notwithftanding when **they are at the** full **perfection, doo debate** and decreafe **againe.**

Cic. de orat. There **is nothing in** the world which **burfteth out** all **at once, and** commeth to light all wholly together.

48. **No** man fhould dare to practife an Arte that is daungerous, efpecially before he haue learned the fame perfectly: fo **doo** guyders **of** Shyppes: fo doo Phifitions: but **fo did not** manie Romaine Poets (yea fo doo not too many Englifh wryters) who in a certaine corragious heate **gaped** after glory by wryting verfes, but fewe **of** them obtayned it.

49. **A Poet fhould be no** leffe fkylfull in dealing with the affectes of **the** mynde, then a tumbler or a Iuggler fhoulde bee ready **in** his Arte. And with fuch pyth fhoulde he fette **foorth hys** matters, that a Reader fhoulde feeme not onely **to** heare **the** thing, but to fee **and** be prefent at the dooing thereof. Which faculty *Fabius* calleth ὑποτασιν and *Ariftotle* προ ομματον θεσιν ἡ ποιησιμ.

50. **Poets are** either **fuch as** defire to be liked of on **ftages, as** Commedie and Tragedie wryters: or fuch as **woulde bee** regeftred **in** Libraries. Thofe on ftages haue fpeciall refpect **to** the motions of the minde, that they **may ftirre bothe** the eyes and eares of their beholders. But **the** other which feeke to pleafe priuately with[in] **the** walles, take good aduifement in their workes, that they may fatiffy the exact iudgments of learned **men in their** ftudies.

51. **A** Poet **fhoulde** not **b**ee too importunate, as to offende in vnfeafonable fpeeches: or vngentle, as to contemne the admonitions of others: or ambicious, as

to thinke too well of his owne dooinges: or too wayward, as to thinke, reward enough cannot be gyuen him for his deferte, or finally too proude, as to defyre to be honoured aboue meafure.

52. The emendations of **Poemes** be very neceffary, that in the obfcure poyntes many thinges may be enlightned, in the bafer partes many thinges may be throughly garnifhed. Hee may take away and put out all vnpropper and vnfeemely words, he may with difcretion immitate the auncient wryters, he may abridge thinges that are too lofty, mittigate thynges that are too rough, and may vfe all remedies of fpeeche throughout the whole worke. The thinges which are fcarce feemely, he may amende by Arte and methode.

53. Let a Poet firft take vppon him, as though he were to play but an Actors part, as he may bee efteemed like one which wryteth without regarde, neyther let him fo pollifh his works, but that euery one for the bafeneffe thereof, may think to make as good. Hee may likewyfe exercife the part of gefturer, as though he feemed to meddle in rude and common matters, and yet not fo deale in them, as it were for variety fake, nor as though he had laboured them thoroughly but tryfled with them, nor as though he had fweat for them, but practifed a little. For fo to hyde ones cunning, that nothing fhould feeme to bee laborfome or exquifite, when notwithftanding, euery part is pollifhed with care and ftudie, is a fpeciall gyft which *Ariftotle* calleth κρῆψν.

54. It is onely a poynt of wyfedome, to vfe many and choyfe elegant words, but to vnderftand alfo and to fet foorth thinges which pertaine to the happy ende of mans life. Whereuppon the Poet *Horace*, calleth the Arte poeticall, without the knowledge of learning and philofophy, a *prating vanity*. Therfore a good and allowable Poet, muft be adorned with wordes, plentious in fentences, and if not equall to an Orator, yet very neere him, and a fpecial louer of learned men.

FINIS.

Epilogus.

His small trauell (courteous Reader) I desire thee take in good worth: which I haue compyled, not as an exquisite censure concerning this matter, but (as thou mayst well perceiue, and) in trueth to that onely ende that it might be an occasion, to haue the same throughly and with greater discretion, taken in hande and laboured by some other of greater abilitie: of whom I knowe there be manie among the famous Poets in London, who bothe for learning and leysure, may handle this Argument far more pythilie then my selfe. Which if any of them wyll vouchsafe to doo, I trust wee shall haue Englishe Poetry at a higher price in short space: and the rabble of balde Rymes shall be turned to famous workes, comparable (I suppose) with the best workes of Poetry in other tongues. In the meane time, if my poore skill, can sette the same any thing forwarde, I wyll not cease to practise the same towardes the framing of some apt English *Prosodia:* styll hoping, and hartelie wishing to enioy first
the benefitte of some others iudgment,
whose authority may beare greater
credite, and whose learn-
ing can better per-
forme it.

(∴)

1 OCTOBER 1870.

Please oblige, by showing this List to your friends.

Works in English Literature

PUBLISHED OR TO BE PUBLISHED BY

EDWARD ARBER,

Associate, King's College, London, F.R.G.S., &c.

AT

QUEEN SQUARE, BLOOMSBURY, LONDON, W.C.

Sold by all Booksellers in the United Kingdom, and by the following, abroad:—

Berlin: N. ASHER.	Montreal: DAWSON BROTHERS.
Bombay: THACKER, VINING & Co.	New York: SCRIBNER, WELFORD & Co.
Boston: LITTLE, BROWN & Co.	Philadelphia: C. J. PRICE.
Calcutta: THACKER, SPINK & Co.	San Francisco: A. L. BANCROFT & Co.
Melbourne: GEORGE ROBERTSON.	Toronto: ADAM, STEVENSON & Co.

*** Foreign booksellers selling these publications can have their names added to the above, in the next List, upon application.

CHRONOLOGICAL LIST.	2

FOR STUDENTS OF ENGLISH LITERATURE.

To STUDENTS.	3
Facsimile Texts.	4
English Reprints, Foolscap size. . . .	5-12
Demy size. . . .	13
Imperial size. . . .	14
Annotated Reprints. (THE PASTON LETTERS.)	15

FOR GENERAL READERS.

Leisure Readings in English Literature. . .	16
Choice Books.	16

These publications are all edited by Mr. Arber, unless otherwise stated.

Any single work may be obtained separately. In ordering quote the NUMBER, SIZE, and PRICE (the author's name is unnecessary).

All orders must be accompanied by a remittance: which, if under 10s., can be made in *Postage Stamps*; if above that sum, in P.O.O., made payable at HIGH HOLBORN Office, or Cheques crossed LONDON AND COUNTY BANK.

These publications are ALWAYS on sale; and may be obtained through your own Bookseller; or, *in any number*, post-free *by return*, on remitting to Mr. ARBER, the Prices, as stated in this List.

The usual allowance to Colleges and Schools.

All inquiries must be accompanied by a Stamp for reply.

Subscriptions, of not less than One Guinea, can be paid in advance of the appearance of the Publications ordered.

This List cancels all previous ones, as regards Works not yet published.

Richard I.
1196. 1486.	*The Revelation to the Monk of Evesham.*		No. 18

Henry VI—Henry VII.
1422–1509.	*The Paston Letters.*		

Henry VIII.
1516, 1566.	Sir T. More. *Utopia.*		14
1527.	W Roy. *Rede me and be nott wrothe.*		
1530	[Roy?] *A proper dyaloge betwene a Gentillman, etc.*		
1545.	R. Ascham. *Toxophilus.*		7

Edward VI.
1549.	Bp. H. Latimer. *The Ploughers.*		12
1549.	Do. *Seven Sermons before Ed. VI.*		13
1550.	Rev. T. Lever. *Sermon in the Shrouds of St. Pauls.*		25
1550.	Do. *Sermon before Ed. VI.*		25
1550.	Do. *Sermon at Pauls Cross.*		25
1553.	N. Udall. *Roister Doister.*		17
1553.	R. Eden. *Translation from S. Munster (1532).*		

Philip and Mary.
1555.	R. Eden. *Translations from Peter Martyr (1516),*		
	Oviedo y Valdes (1521), A. Pigafetta (1532), etc.		
1557.	*Tottel's Miscellany. Songes and Sonettes, etc.*		24

Elizabeth.
1362. 1563.	B. Googe. *Eglogs, Epytaphes, etc.*		23
1570.	R. Ascham. *The Schoolmaster.*		11
1575.	G. Gascoigne. *Notes of Instruction in Eng. verse.*		11
1576.	G. Gascoigne. *The complaynt of Philomene.*		11
1576.	Do. *The Stele Glasse.*		
1577.	G. Whetstone. *A Remembrance of G. Gascoigne.*		11
1579.	J. Lyly. *Euphues. The Anatomy of Wit.*		9
1579.	S. Gosson. *The Schoole of Abuse.*		3
1579.	Do. *An Apologie for the School of Abuse.*		3
1580.	J. Lyly. *Euphues and his England.*		9
1557–1580.	T. Tusser. *Fiue Hundred Points of Good Husbandrie.*		
1582. 1595.	Sir P. Sidney. *An Apologie for Poetrie.*		4
1582.	T. Watson. *The* Ἑκατομπαθία.		21
1583.	Rev. P. Stubbes. *The Anatomie of Abuses.*		
1583.	Do. *2d Part of The Anatomie of Abuses.*		
1586.	James VI. *The Essayes of a Prentise in... Poesie.*		19
1586.	W. Webbe. *A Discourse of English Poetry.*		26
1589.	G. Puttenham. *The Arte of English Poesie.* No. 15		
1590.	Uraldini.—Ryther. *Conceyrynge the Spanishe fleete.*		21
1590.	T. Watson. *Melibæus.*		21
1590.	Do. *An Eclogue, &c.*		6
1590.	E. Webbe. *His Wonderfull Travailes.*		
1591.	Sir W. Ralegh. *The Fight in the 'Revenge.'*		
1592. 1593.	T. Watson. *The Teares of Fancy or Love disdained.*		21
1593.	*The Phœnix Nest.* Ed. by R. S.		
1595.	G. Markham. *The Tragedie of Sir R. Grenville.*		
1597.	F. Bacon. *Essayes.*		

James I.
1604.	[James I.] *A Counterblaste to Tobacco.*		19
1607–12.	Sir F. Bacon. *The Writings, &c. &c.* Harl. MS. 5106.		
1612.	*The Essaies of Sir F. Bacon, Knt.*		
1653.	Sir R. Naunton. *Fragmenta Regalia.*		20

Charles I.
1625.	Francis Lord Verulam. *Essayes or Counsels.*		
1628–33.	Bp. J. Earle. *Microcosmographie.*		12
1625–45.	1689. J. Selden. *Table Talk.*		6
1634–40.	1640. W. Habington. *Castara.*		22
1637.	Star Chamber. *Decree concerning Printing.*		1
1640.	F. Quarles. *Enchyridion.*		
1641.	J. Milton. *The Reason of Church Government, etc.*		
1642.	Do. *Instructions for Forreine Travell.*		16
1643.	J. Milton. *Areopagitica.*		
1644.	Do. *On Education.*		1
1645.	J. Howell. *Epistolæ Ho-Elianæ.* Book I.		
1647.	J. Howell. *Epistolæ Ho-Elianæ.* Book II.		

Commonwealth.
1650.	J. Howell. *Epistolæ Ho-Elianæ.* Book III.		
1650.	Do. *Instructions for travelling, &c. to Turkey.*		18
1655.	Do. *Epistolæ Ho-Elianæ.* Book IV.		

Charles II.
1671. 1672.	G. Villiers, Duke of Buckingham, *The Rehearsal.*		10

William and Mary.
1694.	E. Phillips. *Life of John Milton.*		

Anne.
1712.	J. Addison. *Criticism on Paradise Lost.*		8

URELY to us, after the Sacred Scriptures, works of devotion and of religious instruction; the Literature of England comes next. However exquisite and subtle the charms of Greek and Grecian literature; however necessary and worthy of study the language and literature of Rome; the writings of our Forefathers come home to every Englishman. What a mighty Literature have we inherited! How little is it known, save to a few, who have devoted all their leisure to its exploration! Authors mighty in Prose and Verse! Writers full of aëry fancies and graceful similitudes! Men whose Prose marches with the tramp and strength of a Roman legion: men whose Song is sung by a Puck or an Ariel; or who sing in it of Patient Grissell, of Fair Geraldine, or of Una and her Red Cross Knight. Above all the English Bible, so clung unto by our ancestors—with its infinite early editions and their most heroic story.

What present nation has so ancient, so vast, so varied a body of writings as England? In which are contained not only the productions of our Arch-Poets, Chaucer, Spenser, Shakespeare, Milton, Dryden; but those of an almost uncountable number of authors, inferior indeed to these, but of high rank among ordinary minds.

Good books, besides affording enjoyment, provoke to like excellence. No man writeth unto himself. Each worthy writer is trained, assimilated, and influenced by those who have gone before: each returning a like benefit to posterity. To trace the continuous chain of influence, of cause and effect, link by link, forms a part of the History of English Literature. That History that we may soon hope to possess, for the first time adequately in our language, in Professor HENRY MORLEY's work *English Writers*: of which we have already received the earlier instalment, down to Dunbar. What is designed in the *Facsimile Texts*, the *English Reprints*, and the *Annotated Reprints* is to *represent* the later literature by giving, at as cheap a price as can be, Exact Texts sometimes of books already famous, sometimes of those quite forgotten: in some cases, of works that illustrate the Literary History; in other instances, of those that in a sense, constitute it.

The result is already, that these Reproductions are unique in English Bibliography for their accuracy and cheapness, as well as for the unlimited numbers offered constantly for sale: and *so far as they are yet published*, they constitute the best of all introductions to our old Authors, from the time of Caxton to that of Addison.   E. A.

P.S.—A word in furtherance of the *Early English Text*, the *Chaucer*, and the *Ballad* Societies. No one knows the extent of the unprinted Literature of England. These Societies are recovering for us book after book; and laying us all under great obligation to their able Editors, who labour gratuitously. For further information, apply to F. J. Furnivall, M.A., 3 St. George's Square, London, N.W.

IN VARYING SIZES, FOLLOWING THE ORIGINALS.

F European publications there are not a few which the mere outward appearance, their countenance so to speak, possess an extreme interest. Either from the excessive rarity of the book itself, or the drollery or quaintness of its illustrations; either from the literary importance of the work or its significance in the history of our Country or in the progress of the World: there arises at the sight of it the keenest attention, one might almost say an inexpressible sympathy with the book itself. In all such cases: Sun-Portraits confer exquisite and perpetual enjoyment.

Hitherto Cost has debarred photolithographed books from general use: but I trust to offer from time to time, at *ordinary book-prices*, works of this supreme interest, though necessarily of an infinitely diverse character. In which effort, I trust to receive a thorough support from the large number of readers who have sustained the *English Reprints*. Both being like attempts to make forgotten books known; and known books, more perfectly and perpetually obtainable.

Early in November, will be published in Fcp. 4to., Half Calf, Illuminated sides, pp. xxxii.-64.

[WILLIAM TYNDALE, assisted by WILLIAM ROY.
   The First *printed* English New Testament. Cologne—Worms. 1525. 4to.]

Photo-lithographed, by the permission of the Trustees of the British Museum, from the *unique* fragment in the Grenville Collection.

Briefly told, the story of this profoundly interesting work is as follows:—In 1524 TYNDALE went **from London** to Hamburg; where remaining for about a year, he journeyed on to Cologne: and there assisted by WILLIAM ROY, subsequently the author of the Satire on Wolsey, *Rede me and be nott wrothe* [see p. 11], he began this first edition in 4to; *with glosses* of the English New Testament. A virulent enemy of the Reformation, **COCHLÆUS, at** that time an exile in Cologne, learnt, through giving wine to the printer's men, that P. Quentel the printer had in hand a secret edition of three thousand copies of the English **New** Testament. In great alarm, he informed Herman Rinck, Senator of the **city, who** moved the Senate to stop the printing; but Cochlæus could neither obtain **a sight of** the Translators, nor a sheet of the impression.

Tyndale **and Roy, fled** with the printed sheets, up the Rhine to Worms; and there completing **this edition,** produced also another in Octavo, *without glosses*. Both editions were in England **in** Jan.-March, 1526: **and of** the six thousand copies of which they together were composed, there **remain but** this fragment of the First commenced edition; **and** of the Second edition, **one** complete copy in the Library of **the Baptist College at Bristol, and an imperfect one in** that of St. Paul's Cathedral, **London.**

The price of this *Facsimile Text*, will be only SIX SHILLINGS.

English Reprints.

THE great importance to the increasing study of English Literature, of constantly adding to, and constantly keeping on sale (a more difficult task than at first would appear) at the lowest practicable prices, these Exact Texts; has led to a full consideration of the past three years' progress, in an experiment which has been successful beyond anticipation. The following alterations have been found advisable, in order to place this designedly very cheap **Series upon a permanent basis**.

The changes to take effect from 1st October **1870**.

Small Paper, in Foolscap Octavo.

1. The public **choice** has passed so generally **from** *Cut* to *Uncut* edges: that future issues will be in *Uncut* edges only. This will also apply to all reimpressions, as soon as the existing *Cut-edged* copies have been sold.

2. No **Sixpenny** Reprints will be issued in future. The trouble is out of all proportion to the price.

3. The *maximum* number of pages for Shilling works will be about One hundred and twenty-eight. **Experience has** proved that number to be the *very utmost* limit practicable **for such** closely packed works in the costly old spelling, &c.

∴ The result of these changes to the public will be simply, that some future Reprints will be increased in price, by an extra Sixpence. A trifling contribution to enable me to go on for years. Yet I very reluctantly decide on this augmentation: this series being my personal free offering to a more perfect knowledge of English Literature.

All existing issues will be maintained at the present prices.

Large Paper, in Foolscap Quarto.

Nos. 19 to 24 in Large Paper are now ready. A single **Large Paper** copy can be obtained.

Demy Quarto.

Works in this size will be issued bound in Cloth. When published, **copies** will however be obtainable in Sheets, for binding, by remitting the price *direct* to me.

There is a great cause for thankfulness in the progress already made. Works which some of **our** most experienced English scholars never hoped **to see** reprinted; have been put into *general* circulation. Much more may be **accomplished**, by a personal advocacy of this Series by *each* Purchaser; **with a** generous permission to print, from possessors of **rare or** unique English books; and with unwearying effort on my own **part.** Maintaining herein the ancient **and** worthy fame of England; **may** we lead very many to understand how much pure and unadulterated Delight is to be found **in our** Old English Authors.

English Reprints.

ORDINARY ISSUE IN OCTAVO.
Durable Cases, in Roxburghe style, to hold four or five **Reprints.** One Shilling each.

BOUND VOLUMES IN OCTAVO.
Two or three of such works, collected into occasional Volumes.

LARGE PAPER EDITION IN QUARTO.
The same texts, beautifully printed on thick toned paper, with **ample** *margins suitable for purposes of study. Issued in Stiff covers, uncut edges.* **When** *bound to the purchaser's* **own** *taste ; these Large Paper Copies form most handsome books.*

ANY SINGLE WORK OR VOLUME MAY BE HAD SEPARATELY.

Quarto.	FOOLSCAP.	Octavo.
Large Paper Edit.		Stiff Covers. Uncut Edges. / Green Cloth, Red Edges.
	1. JOHN MILTON.	
	(1) A decree of the Starre-Chamber, concerning Printing, **made** the eleuenth day of July last past. London, 1637.	
	(2) An Order of the Lords and Commons assembled in Parliament for the regulating of Printing, &c. London, 14 June, 1643.	
1/6	(3) *AREOPAGITICA :* A speech of Mr. John Milton for the liberty of Vnlicenc'd Printing, to the Parliament of England. London. [24 November]. 1644. Sixpence.	Vol. I.
	2. HUGH LATIMER, *Ex-Bishop of Worcester.*	Milton,
1/6	*SERMON ON* **THE** *PLOUGHERS.* A notable Sermon of ye reuerende father Master Hughe Latimer, whiche he preached in ye Shrouds at paules churche in London, on the xviii daye of Januarye. ☾ The yere of our Loorde MDXLviii. Sixpence.	Latimer, Gosson
	3. STEPHEN GOSSON, *Stud. Oxon.*	2/
	(1) *THE SCHOOLE OF ABUSE.* Conteining a pleasaunt invective against Poets, Pipers, Plaiers, **Jesters,** and such like Caterpillers of a Commonwealth ; Setting **up the** Flagge of Defiance to their mischievous exercise, and ouerthrowing their Bulwarkes, by Prophane Writers, **Naturall reason, and common** experience. A discourse as pleasaunt **for** gentlemen that fauour learning, as profitable for all **that** wyll follow vertue. London. [August ?] 1579.	
1/6	(2) *AN APOLOGIE OF THE SCHOOLE OF ABUSE,* against Poets, **Pipers,** and their Excusers. London. [December ?] 1579. Sixpence.	
	4. SIR PHILIP SYDNEY.	
1/6	*AN APOLOGIE* **FOR** *POETRIE.* Written by the right noble, vertuous **and** learned Sir Philip Sidney, Knight. London, 1595. Sixpence.	

ENGLISH REPRINTS—FOOLSCAP.   7

Quarto. Large Paper Edit.	TITLES, PRICES, etc., etc.	Octavo. Stiff Covers. Uncut Edges.	Green Cloth, Red Edges.
	5. EDWARD WEBBE, *Chief Master Gunner.*		
1/6	The rare and most vvonderful thinges which Edward Webbe an Englishman borne, hath seene and passed in his troublesome trauailes, in the Citties of Ierusalem, Damasko, Bethelem, and Galely: and in the Landes of Iewrie, Egipt, Gtecia, Russia, and in the land of Prester Iohn. Wherein is set foorth his extreame slauerie sustained many yeres togither, in the Gallies and wars of the great Turk against the Landes of Persia, Tartaria, Spaine, and Portugall, with the manner of his releasement, and comming into London in May last. London. 1590. Sixpence.	**Vol. II.** Sidney, Webbe, Selden. 2/6	
2/6	**6. JOHN SELDEN.** *TABLE TALK:* being the Discourses of John Seldon Esq.; or his Sence of various Matters of Weight and High Consequence relating especially to Religion and State. London. 1689. One Shilling.		
2/6	**7. ROGER ASCHAM.** *TOXOPHILUS.* The schole of shooting conteyned in tvvo bookes. To all Gentlemen and yomen of Englande, pleasaunte for theyr pastime to rede, and profitable for theyr use to folow, both in warre and peace. London. 1545. One Shilling.	**Vol. III.** Ascham, Addison. 2/6	
2/6	**8. JOSEPH ADDISON.** *CRITICISMS OF MILTON'S PARADISE LOST.* From *The Spectator:* being its Saturday issues between 31 December, 1711, and 3 May, 1712. One Shilling.		
9/	**9. JOHN LYLY, M.A.** (1) ☞ *EUPHUES. THE ANATOMY OF WIT.* Verie pleasaunt for all Gentlemen to read, and most necessarie to remember. Wherein are contained the delightes that Wit followeth in his youth by the pleasantnesse of loue, and the happinesse he reapeth in age, by the perfectnesse of Wisedome. London. 1579. (2) ☞ *EUPHUES AND HIS ENGLAND.* Containing his voyage and aduentures, myxed with sundrie pretie discourses of honest Loue, the Description of the Countrey, the Court, and the manners of that Isle. Delightful to be read, and nothing hurtful to be regarded: wher-in there is small offence by lightnesse giuen to the wise, and lesse occasion of loosenes proferred to the wanton. London, 1580. Collated with early subsequent editions. Four Shillings.	**Vol. IV.** Lyly. 5/	

ENGLISH REPRINTS—FOOLSCAP.

Quarto. Large Paper Edit	TITLES, PRICES, etc., etc.	Octavo. Stiff Covers. Uncut Edges.	Green Cloth, Red Edges.
2/6	**10. GEORGE VILLIERS,** *Duke of Buckingham.* THE REHEARSAL. As it was acted at the Theatre Royal London, 1672. With Illustrations from previous plays, &c. **One Shilling.**		Vol. V. Villiers, Gascoigne, Earle. 3/6
2/6	**11. GEORGE GASCOIGNE,** *Esquire.* (1) A remembravnce of the wel imployed life, and godly end of George Gaskoigne, Esquire, who deceassed at Stalmford in Lincoln shire, the 7 of October 1577. The reporte of GEOR WHETSTONS, Gent an eye witness of his Godly and Charitable End in this world. Lond. 1577. (2) Certayne notes of Instruction concerning the making of verse or rime in English, vvritten at the request of Master *Edouardi Donati.* 1575. (3) *THE STEELE GLAS.* A Satyre compiled by George Gasscoigne Esquire [Written between Apr. 1575 & Apr. 1576]. Together with (4) *THE COMPLAYNT OF PHYLOMENE.* An Elegie compyled by George Gasscoigne Esquire [between April 1562 and 3rd April 1575.] London. 1576. **One Shilling.**		
2/6	**12. JOHN EARLE, M.A.** : *afterwards in succession Bishop of Worcester, and of Salisbury.* MICRO-COSMOGRAPHIE, or a Peece of the World discovered, in Essays and Characters. London. 1628. With the additions in subsequent editions during the Author's life time. **One Shilling.**		
4/	**13. HUGH LATIMER,** *Ex-Bishop of Worcester.* SEVEN SERMONS BEFORE EDWARD VI. (1) ¶ The fyrste sermon of Mayster Hugh Latimer, whiche he preached before the Kynges Maiest. wythin his graces palayce at Westmynster. M.D.XLIX. the viii of Marche. (,‘,) (2) The seconde [to seventh] Sermon of Master Hughe Latimer, whych he preached before the Kynges maiestic, withyn hys graces Palayce at Westminster ye. xv. day of March. M.cccc.xlix. **Eighteen Pence.**		Vol. VI. Latimer, More. 3/
2/6	**14. SIR THOMAS MORE.** UTOPIA. A frutefull pleasaunt, and wittie worke, of the best state of a publique weale, and of the new yle, called Utopia : written in Latine, by the right worthie and famous Sir Thomas More knyght, and translated into Englishe by RAPHE ROBYNSON, sometime fellowe of Corpus Christi College in Oxford, and nowe by him at this seconde edition newlie perused and corrected, and also with diuers notes in the margent augmented. London. [1556]. **One Shilling.**		

ENGLISH REPRINTS—FOOLSCAP.

Quarto. Large Paper Edit.	TITLES, PRICES, etc., etc.	Octavo.

5/ **15. GEORGE PUTTENHAM.** *Stiff Covers. Uncut Edges.*
THE ARTE OF ENGLISH POESIE. Contriued into three Bookes : The first of Poets and Poesie, the second of Proportion, the third of Ornament. London. 1589. **Two Shillings.**

Green Cloth, Red Edges.
Vol. VII.
Puttenham.
2/6

1/6 **16. JAMES HOWELL,** *Historiographer Royal to Charles II.*
INSTRUCTIONS FOR FORREINE TRAVELL. Shewing by what *cours*, and in what *compasse of time*, one may take an exact Survey of the Kingdomes and States of Christendome, and arriue to the practicall knowledge of the Languages, to good purpose. London. 1642. Collated with the edition of 1656 ; and in its 'new Appendix for Travelling into *Turkey* and the *Levant* parts' added. **Sixpence.**

Vol. VIII.

1/6 **17. The earliest known English comedy.**
NICHOLAS UDALL, *Master of Eton.*
ROISTER DOISTER, [from the unique copy at Eton College]. 1566. **Sixpence.**

Howell.
Udall.

2/6 **18.** *THE REVELATION TO THE MONK OF EVESHAM.* Here begynnyth a marvelous revelacion that was schewyd of almighty god by sent Nycholas to a monke of Euyshamme yn the days of Kynge Richard the fyrst. And the yere of our lord, M.C.Lxxxxvi. [From the unique copy, printed abont 1482, in the British Museum]. **One Shilling.**

Monk of Evesham
James VI.
3/6

2/6 **19. JAMES VI.** *of Scotland,* **I.** *of England.*
(1) *THE ESSAYES OF A PRENTISE, IN THE DIVINE ART OF POESIE.* Edinburgh 1585.
(2) *A COUNTER BLASTE TO TOBACCO.* London. 1604. **One Shilling.**

1/6 **20. SIR ROBERT NAUNTON,** *Master of the Court of Wards.*
FRAGMENTA REGALIA : or, Observations on the late Queen Elizabeth, her Times, and Favourites. [Third Edition. London] 1653. **Sixpence.**

Vol. IX.

21. THOMAS WATSON, *Student at law.*
(1) *THE* Ἑκατομπαθία *or Passionate Centurie of Loue. Divided into two parts: whereof, the first expresseth the Authors sufferance in Loue: the* **latter,** *his long farewell to Loue and all his tyrannie.* Composed by *Thomas Watson* Gentleman ; and published at the request of certaine Gentlemen his very **frendes.** London [1582].

Naunton.
Watson.
2/6

ENGLISH REPRINTS—FOOLSCAP.

Quarto. Large Paper Edit.	TITLES, PRICES, etc., etc.	Octavo. Stiff Covers. Uncut Edges.	Green Cloth. Red Edges.
4/	(2) *MELIBŒUS* T. Watsoni, Ecloga in obitum F. Walsinghami, &c. Londini, 1590. (3) *AN EGLOGUE*, &c., Written first in latine [the above MELIBŒUS] by *Thomas Watson* Gentleman and now by himselfe translated into English. London 1590. (4) *THE TEARS OF FANCY*, or Loue disdained. [From the unique copy, wanting Sonnets ix.-xvi., in the possession of S. Christie-Miller, Esq.] London, 1593. Eighteen Pence.		
2/6	**22. WILLIAM HABINGTON.** *CASTARA.* The third Edition. Corrected and augmented. London. 1640. With the variations of the two previous editions. One Shilling.		Vol. X? Habington.
2/6	**23. ROGER ASCHAM.** *THE SCHOLEMASTER*, Or plaine and perfite way of teachyng children, to vnderstand, write, and speake, the Latin tong, but specially purposed for the priuate bryngyng vp of youth in Ientlemen and Noble mens houses, commodious also for all such, as haue forgot the Latin tongue, and would, by themselues, without a Scholemaster, in short tyme, and with small paines, recouer a sufficient habilitie, to vnderstand, write, and speake Latin. London. 1570. One Shilling.		Ascham. 2/6
6/6	**24. Tottel's Miscellany.** *SONGES AND SONETTES*, written by the ryght honorable Lorde, HENRY HAWARD, late Erle of Surrey, and other. [London, 5 June] 1557. Half-a-crown.		Vol. XI. Tottel. 3/
4/	**25. REV. THOMAS LEVER, M.A.**: *afterwards Master of St John's College, Cambridge.* *SERMONS.* (1) A fruitfull Sermon made in Paules churche at London in the Shroudes, the second of Februari. 1550. (2) A Sermon preached the thyrd [or fourth] Sunday in Lent before the Kynges Maiestie, and his honourable counsell. 1550. (3) A Sermon preached at Pauls Crosse, the xiiii. day of December 1550. Eighteen Pence.		Vol. XII. Lever.
2/6	**26. WILLIAM WEBBE,** *Graduate.* *A DISCOURSE OF ENGLISH POETRIE.* Together, with the Authors judgment, touching the reformation of our English Verse. London. 1586. One Shilling.		Webbe. 3/

∴ *The following works are designed for publication in time to come. Their prices cannot be fixed with precision, but are approximately* **given.** Ferrex and **Porrex** *has been postponed; and*

Newes from the North by F. T. [FRANCIS THYNNE], *with* RICHARD BARNFIELD's Poems *have not been inserted; some of the Texts not being accessible, at the present time.* J. HOWELL'S Epistolæ Ho-Elianæ *will be put to press as soon as No.* 27 BACON'S Essayes, &c., *is finished.*

Large Paper Edit.			
	27. FRANCIS BACON. *Stiff Covers. Uncut Edges.*		*Green Cloth, Red Ed₄ es.*
	A harmony of the *ESSAYES*, &c.		
	The four principle texts appearing in parallel columns. ;		
	(1) Essayes. Religious Meditations. Places of perswasion and disswasion. London 1597. (10 Essays.)		Vol. XIII.
	Of the Coulers of good and euill a fragment. 1597.		
	(2) The writings of Sir Francis Bacon Knt : the Kinges Sollicitor Generall : in Moralitie, Policie, and Historic. *Harleian MS.* 5106. Transcribed bet. 1607-12. (34 Essays.)		Bacon.
	(3) THE ESSAIES of Sir FRANCIS BACON Knight, the Kings Solliciter Generall. London 1612. (38 Essays.)		3/6
7/6	(4) The Essayes or Counsels, Ciuill and Morall, of FRANCIS LO. VERULAM Viscount ST. ALBANS. *Newly Written.* 1626. (58 Essays.) Three Shillings.		
	28. WILLIAM ROY, *Franciscan Friar.*		
	(1) *REDE ME AND BE NOTT WROTHE.* [Strasburg. 1527. This is his famous Satire on Wolsey.]		
2/6	(2) *A PROPER DYALOGE BETWEEN A GENTLEMAN AND A HUSBANDMAN,* &c. [Attributed to Roy] Marburg. 1530. Eighteen Pence.		Vol. XIV.
	29. SIR W. RALEIGH—G. MARKHAM.		Roy.
	THE LAST FIGHT OF THE REVENGE AT SEA. (1) A report of the Truth of the fight about the Isles of Acores, this last Sommer. Betvvixt the Reuenge, one of her Maiesties Shippes, and an Armada of the King of Spaine. By Sir Walter Raleigh. London. 1591.		Fight in the Revenge.
	(2) The most Honorable Tragedie of Sir Richarde Grinuille, Knight (∵) *Bramo assai, poco spero, nulla chieggio.* [By GERVASE MARKHAM] London. 1595.		Googe.
2/6	[Two copies only are known, Mr. Grenville's cost £40.] One Shilling.		4/
	30. BARNABE GOOGE.		
2/6	*EGLOGS, EPYTAPHES AND SONETTES* newly written by Barnabe Googe. London 1563. 15 March. One Shilling.		
	31. REV. PHILLIP STUBBES.		
	(1) *THE ANATOMIE OF ABUSES:* conteyning a discouerie or briefe Summarie of Such Notable Vices and Imperfections, as now raigne in many Christian		

ENGLISH REPRINTS—FOOLSCAP.

Quarto. Large Paper Edit.	TITLES, PRICES, etc., etc.	Octavo. Stiff Covers. Uncut Edges.	Green Cloth, Red Edges.
6/6	Countreyes of the World : but especialie in a very famous ILANDE called AILGNA [i.e. Anglia]: Together with most fearefull Examples of Gods Iudgementes, executed vpon the wicked for the same, aswell in AILGNA of late, as in other places, elsewhere. . . London. 1 Maij. 1583. (2) The Second part of *THE ANATOMIE OF ABUSES*. . . . London. 1583. Half-a-crown.		Vol. Stubbes. 3/
	32. THOMAS TUSSER. *FIVE HUNDRED POINTES OF GOOD HUS- BANDRIE*, as well for the Champion, or open Countrie, as also for the woodland, or Seuerall, mixed in euery Month with *HUSWIFERIE*, . . . with diuers other lessons, as a diet for the former, of the properties of windes, plantes, hops, herbes, bees and approued re- medies for sheepe and cattle, with many other matters both profitable and not vnpleasant for the Reader . .		Vol.
4/	. . London. 1580. Eighteen Pence.		Tusser.
2/6	**33. JOHN MILTON.** (1) The Life of Mr John Milton [by his nephew EDWARD PHILLIPS]. From '*Letters of State written by Mr. John Milton*, bet. 1649-59.' London. 1694. (2) *THE REASON OF CHURCH GOVERNE- MENT* urg'd against Prelacy. By Mr. *John Milton*. In two Books. [London] 1641. (3) Milton's Letter *OF EDUCATION*. To Master *Samuel Hartlib*. [London. 5 June 1644.] One Shilling.		Milton. 3/
2/6	**34. FRANCIS QUARLES.** *ENCHYRIDION*, containing Insti- tuti- ons { Divine { Contemplative. Practicall. Ethycall. Morall { Oeconomicall. Politicall. London. 1640-1. One Shilling.		Vol. Quarles.
2/6	**35. The Sixth English Poetical Miscellany.** *THE PHOENIX NEST*. Built vp with the most rare and refined workes of Noble men, woorthy Knights, gallant Gentlemen, Masters of Arts, and braue Schoolers. Full of varietie, excellent inuention, and singular delight. *Never before this time published*. Set forth by R. S. of the Inner Temple Gentleman. London 1593. One Shilling.		The Phœ- nix Nest. 2/6
6/6	**36. SIR THOMAS ELYOT.** *THE GOVERNOR*. The boke named the Gouernor, deuised by ye Thomas Elyot Knight. Londini M.D.xxxi. Collated with subsequent editions. Half-a-crown.		Vol. Elyot. 3/

Demy Quarto.

Will be ready, about March 1871, in one Volume, 12s. 6d.

801. RICHARD EDEN.

I. A treatyse *OF THE NEWE INDIA, WITH OTHER NEW FOUNDE LANDES AND ISLANDS, ASWELL EASTWARDE AS WESTWARDE*, as they are knowen and found in these oure dayes, after the descripcion of SEBASTIAN MUNSTER, in his boke of vniuersall Cosmographie, &c. [London, 1553.]

II. The First English Collection of Voyages, Traffics, and Discoveries.—*THE DECADES OF THE NEW WORLD OR WEST INDIA, &c. &c.* [by Peter Martyr of Angleria.] [Translated, compiled, &c. by Richard Eden.] Londini, Anno 1555.

1. The [Dedicatory] Epistle [to King Philip and Queen Mary.]
2. Richard Eden to the Reader.
3. The [1st, 2nd, and 3d only of the 8] Decades of the newe worlde or west India, Conteynyng the nauigations and conquestes of the Spanyardes, with the particular description of the moste ryche and large lands and Ilandes lately founde in the west Ocean perteynyng to the inheritance of the kinges of Spayne. In the which the diligent reader may not only consyder what commoditie may hereby chaunce to the hole christian world in tyme to come, but also learne many secreates touchynge the lande, the sea, and the starres, very necessarie to be knowen to al such as shal attempte any nauigations, or otherwise haue delite to beholde the strange and woonderful woorkes of god and nature. Wrytten in the Latine tounge by PETER MARTYR of Angleria, and translated into Englysshe by RYCHARDE EDEN.
4. The Bull of Pope Alexander VI. in 1493, granting to the Spaniards 'the Regions and Ilandes founde in the Weste Ocean' by them.
5. *The Historie of the West Indies* by GONÇALO FERNANDEZ OVIEDO Y VALDES.
6. Of other notable things gathered out of dyuers autors.
7. Of Moscouie and Cathay.
8. Other notable thynges as touchynge the Indies [chiefly out of the books of FRANCISCO LOPEZ DE GOMARA, 'and partly also out of the caade made by SEBASTIAN CABOT.']
9. The Booke of Metals.
10. The description of the two viages made owt of England into Guinea in Affricke [1553, 1554].
11. The maner of fyndynge the Longitude of regions.

INDEX.

.·. An abridged analysis of this voluminous work was issued in the previous catalogue (1 Dec. 1869); which will be found bound up with 'English Reprints' issued during this year, 1870.

Imperial Folio.

1001. PETRUCCIO UBALDINI—AUGUSTIN RYTHER.

A Discourse concerning the Spanishe fleete inuading Englande in the yeare 1588 and ouerthrowne by her Maieties Nauie vnder the conduction of the Right-honorable the Lorde Charles Howarde highe Admirall of Englande, written in Italian by PETRUCCIO VBALDINI citizen of Floence, and translated for A. RYTHER: vnto the which discourse are annexed certain tables expressinge the generall exploites and conflictes had with the said fleete.

These bookes with the tables belonginge to them are to be solde at the shoppe of A. RYTHER, being a little from Leaden hall next to the Signe of the Tower. [1590.]

The twelve Tables express the following subjects:—

FRONTISPIECE.

I. THE SPANISH ARMADA COMING INTO THE CHANNEL, OPPOSITE THE LIZARD; AS IT WAS FIRST DISCOVERED.

II. THE SPANISH ARMADA AGAINST FOWEY, DRAWN UP IN THE FORM OF A HALF MOON; THE ENGLISH FLEET PURSUING.

III. THE FIRST ENGAGEMENT BETWEEN THE TWO FLEETS, AFTER WHICH THE ENGLISH GIVE CHASE TO THE SPANIARDS, WHO DRAW THEIR SHIPS INTO A BALL.

IV. DE VALDEZ'S GALLEON SPRINGS HER FOREMAST, AND IS TAKEN BY SIR FRANCIS DRAKE. THE LORD ADMIRAL WITH THE 'BEAR' AND THE 'MARY ROSE,' PURSUE THE ENEMY, WHO SAIL IN THE FORM OF A HALF MOON.

V. THE ADMIRAL'S SHIP OF THE GUIPUSCOAN SQUADRON HAVING CAUGHT FIRE, IS TAKEN BY THE ENGLISH. THE ARMADA CONTINUES ITS COURSE, IN A HALF MOON; UNTIL OFF THE ISLE OF PORTLAND, WHERE ENSUES THE SECOND ENGAGEMENT.

VI. SOME ENGLISH SHIPS ATTACK THE SPANIARDS TO THE WESTWARD. THE ARMADA AGAIN DRAWING INTO A BALL, KEEPS ON ITS COURSE FOLLOWED BY THE ENGLISH.

VII. THE THIRD AND THE SHARPEST FIGHT BETWEEN THE TWO FLEETS: OFF THE ISLE OF WIGHT.

VIII. THE ARMADA SAILING UP CHANNEL TOWARDS CALAIS; THE ENGLISH FLEET FOLLOWING CLOSE.

IX. THE SPANIARDS AT ANCHOR OFF CALAIS. THE FIRESHIPS APPROACHING. THE ENGLISH PREPARING TO PURSUE.

X. THE FINAL BATTLE. THE ARMADA FLYING TO THE NORTHWARD. THE CHIEF GALLEASS STRANDED NEAR CALAIS.

LARGE MAP SHOWING THE TRACK OF THE ARMADA ROUND THE BRITISH ISLES.

These plates, which are a most valuable and early representation of the Spanish Invasion, are being re-engraved in *facsimile*, and will be issued in the Spring of 1877, at the lowest feasible price: probably HALF-A-GUINEA.

∴ *Other works* **may follow.**

Annotated Reprints.

By various Editors: under Mr. Arber's General Supervision.

Some Texts require the amplest elucidation and illustration by Masters in special departments of knowledge. To recover and perpetuate such Works is to render the greatest service to Learning. With the aid of Scholars in special subjects, I hope to endow our readers with some knowledge of the Past, that is now quite out of their reach. While the Editors will be responsible both for Text and Illustrations; the works will be produced under my general oversight: so that the Annotated Reprints, though of much slower growth, will more than equal in value the English Reprints.

E. A.

In the Spring of 1871: in Fcp. 8vo the First Volume (to be completed in Four) of

The Paston Letters. 1422-1509.

Edited by JAMES GAIRDNER, Esq., of the Public Record Office.

EVERY one knows what a blank is the history of England during the Wars of the two Roses. Amid the civil commotions, literature almost died out. The principal poetry of the period is that of Lydgate, the Monk of Bury. The prose still more scanty. The monastic Chronicles are far less numerous than at earlier periods: and by the end of the Fifteenth Century they seem to have entirely ceased. Thus it has come to pass that less is known of this age than of any other in our history. In this general dearth of information recent historians like Lingard, Turner, Pauli, and Knight, who have treated of the reigns of Henry VI., Edward IV., &c., have found in *The Paston Letters* not only unrivalled illustration of the Social Life of England, but also most important information, at first hand, as to the Political events of that time. So that the printed Correspondence is cited page after page in their several histories of this period.

The Paston Letters have not however been half published. No literary use was made of them while accumulating in the family muniment room. William, 2nd Earl of Yarmouth, the last member of the family, having encumbered his inheritance, parted with all his property. The family letters came about 1728 into the hands of the distinguished antiquary, Peter le Neve; afterwards, by his marriage to Le Neve's widow, to his brother antiquary Martin of Palgrave; on his death again, to a Mr. Worth, from whom they were acquired by Mr. afterwards Sir John Fenn.

In 1787, Fenn published a small selection of the Letters in two volumes 4to; of which the first edition having been sold off in a week, a second appeared in the course of the year. He then prepared a further selection, of which two volumes appeared in 1789; the fifth volume being published after his death, in 1823.

Strangely enough, the Original Letters disappeared soon after their publication: and only those of the Fifth volume have, as yet, been recovered. There is no reasonable doubt that they still exist and will some day be found. There is no necessity, however, to postpone a new edition indefinitely, until they are again brought to light: for a comparison of the Fifth volume with its originals establishes Sir John Fenn's general faithfulness as to the Text; and therefore our present possession, in his Edition, of the contents of the missing Manuscripts.

Three hundred and eighty-seven letters in all were published by Fenn: about four hundred additional letters or documents, belonging to the same collection and which have never been published at all, will be included in the present edition.

Not only will the Text be doubled in quantity; but in its elucidation, it will have the benefit of Mr. Gairdner's concentrated study of this Correspondence for years past. Half his difficulty will be in the unravelling of the chronology of the Letters, partly from internal evidence, partly from the Public Records, and other sources. Fenn's chronology—for no fault of his—is excessively misleading. This was inevitable, from the difficulties of a first attempt, the state of historic criticism in his day, and the limited means then available for consulting the public records, &c. It is hoped, however, by restoring each Letter to its certain or approximate date, vastly to increase the interest of this Correspondence. In addition textual difficulties will be removed, and valuable biographical information afforded.

The Letters of the reign of Henry VI. will form Vol. I. (estimated at about 600 pp.): those of Edward IV., Vols. II. and III. (together about 800 pp.): and those of Richard III. and Henry VII., Vol. IV. (about 300 pp.). The price will be *about one shilling for every 100 pp.*; and the work, it is expected, will be completed in Two years.

THE undermentioned modernized texts are in preparation. Great care will be bestowed in their transformation into the spelling and punctuation of the present day: but the Originals will be adhered to as closely as possible.

Leisure Readings in English Literature.

The object of the volumes that will appear under this general title, will be to afford Restful Reading; and, at the same time, by exhibiting the wealth of thought and the wit in expression of our Old Authors; to predispose to a further study of our Literature: in which study these Readings will serve as First Books.

They will contain many excellent Poems and Passages that are generally but very little known.

Choice Books.

THE DISASTROUS ENGLISH VOYAGE TO THE WEST INDIES IN 1568.

Recounted in the Narratives of Sir JOHN HAWKINS: and of DAVID INGRAM, MILES PHILLIPS, and JOB HORTOP, survivors, who escaped through the American Indian tribes; or out of the clutches of the Inquisition; or from the galleys of the King of Spain: and so at length came home to England.

∴ *Other works to follow.*

These works will be issued, beautifully printed and elegantly bound, in Crown 8vo.
The above is a specimen of the type, but not of the size of page.

---

5 QUEEN SQUARE, BLOOMSBURY, LONDON, W.C.

www.ingramcontent.com/pod-product-compliance
Lightning Source LLC
Chambersburg PA
CBHW031619170426
43195CB00037B/1212